THE
BOX
OF
STARS

THE
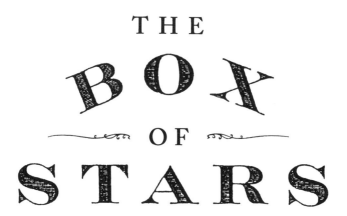
BOX
OF
STARS

A PRACTICAL GUIDE
TO THE NIGHT SKY
AND TO ITS
MYTHS & LEGENDS

CATHERINE TENNANT

A Bulfinch Press Book
Little, Brown and Company
Boston • New York • London

First North American Edition
Ninth Printing, 2000
Designed by Terry Jeavons

First published in the United Kingdom in 1993 by
Chatto & Windus
Random House, 20 Vauxhall Bridge Road, London SW1V 2SA

ISBN 0-8212-2038-1

Bulfinch Press is an imprint and trademark of
Little, Brown and Company (Inc.)

PRINTED IN CHINA

CONTENTS

Introduction 1

How to Use the Cards............................... 6

The Maps.. 7

The Lettering on the Cards....................... 7

From the Northern Hemisphere 8

    The Circumpolar Stars................................. 8

    The Stars in Winter.................................... 9

    The Stars in Spring..................................... 10

    The Stars in Summer.................................. 11

    The Stars in Autumn.................................. 12

From the Southern Hemisphere........................ 13

    The Stars in Summer.................................. 13

    The Stars in Autumn.................................. 14

    The Stars in Winter.................................... 15

    The Stars in Spring..................................... 16

Plate 1   Draco and Ursa Minor....................... 18

Plate 2   Camelopardalis, Tarandus and
Custos Messium................................. 20

Plate 3   Cassiopeia.. 21

Plate 4   Cepheus... 22

Plate 5   Gloria Frederici, Andromeda
and Triangula..................................... 23

Plate 6   Perseus and Caput Medusae.............. 25

Plate 7   Auriga... 27

Plate 8   Lynx and Telescopium Herschilii...... 29

Plate 9   Ursa Major... 30

Plate 10 Boötes, Canes Venatici,
Coma Berenices and
Quadrans Muralis.............................. 32

Plate 11 Hercules and Corona Borealis............. 34

Plate 12 Taurus Poniatowski, Serpentarius,
Scutum Sobiesky and Serpens............ 37

Plate 13 Delphinus, Sagitta, Aquila and
Antinous.. *40*

Plate 14 Lacerta, Cygnus, Lyra, Vulpecula
and Anser.. *43*

Plate 15 Pegasus and Equuleus......................... *46*

Plate 16 Aries and Musca Borealis.................... *48*

Plate 17 Taurus.. *50*

Plate 18 Gemini.. *52*

Plate 19 Cancer.. *54*

Plate 20 Leo Major and Leo Minor.................. *56*

Plate 21 Virgo.. *58*

Plate 22 Libra.. *60*

Plate 23 Scorpio.. *62*

Plate 24 Sagittarius and Corona Australis
with Microscopium
and Telescopium................................ *64*

Plate 25 Capricornus.. *66*

Plate 26 Aquarius, Piscis Australis and
Ballon Aerostatique............................ *68*

Plate 27 Pisces.. *71*

Plate 28 Psalterium Georgii, Fluvius
Eridanus, Cetus, Officina
Sculptoris, Fornax Chemica
and Machina Electrica....................... *73*

Plate 29 Orion.. *76*

Plate 30 Canis Major, Lepus, Columba Noachi
and Cela Sculptoris............................ *78*

Plate 31 Monoceros, Canis Minor and
Atelier Typographique........................ *80*

Plate 32 Noctua, Corvus, Crater,
Sextans Uraniae, Hydra, Felis, Lupus,
Centaurus, Antlia Pneumatica,
Argo Navis and Pyxis Nautica............ *82*

INTRODUCTION

Star-gazing is one of the oldest human occupations. To locate the ancient constellations, many of them forty or fifty centuries old, is to see the world through the eyes of our earliest known ancestors, to re-enter the Bronze Age 'DreamTime', when the myths, the mysterious, primordial images in man's psyche, were first placed in the skies.

The stars themselves, of course, have been there from time immemorial, but of the eighty-eight official man-made constellations, which were finalised worldwide in 1930, forty-eight were listed by Ptolemy in the second century AD. The skies are alive with symbols and, from Orion, the Hunter, the handsomest man in the world who went blind but regained his sight by looking at the sunrise, to Serpentarius, the Healer, holding the serpent of medicine and rebirth, and Boötes, the Herdsman, who pursues the Bears around the pole, they all tell their own story of a timeless world. Modern science also tells us that the glittering firmament which surrounds us is timeless in another way as well. Until the sixteenth century men believed that the stars which they grouped into constellations were near to us and to each other, but we now know that centuries often lie between the moments at which the individual stars give out their light, and that the universe is boundless, and populated with black holes and spinning galaxies.

In this booklet, which is not intended to be a scientific guide, I have tried to bring together these two completely different ways of looking at the skies. Under the heading of each card, I have first given the myths and legends associated with each constellation, and then, in 'The Stars', not only the stories and beliefs connected with the individual stars, but any scientific information which seems to add to the sense of awe and wonder with which we view the universe we live in. Lastly, comes a section headed 'To Locate' which, when used with the maps and the description of the sky, by season, enables you to find the constellation in the sky.

In the ancient world, star worship was almost universal. Nearly everywhere, the Milky Way was seen as the pathway along which the dead returned to their true home in the immortal stars, and even to Aristotle and Cicero, they were divine. The early Christians saw them as living beings; the Cherubims being the fixed stars, and, far earlier, temples and tombs, such as the great pyramid at Ghizeh and the temple to the many-breasted Diana of Ephesus, in Turkey, were built in alignment with them. According to one Greek writer of the fourth century AD, they are the source of all mythology: 'The ancients believed that the legends of Osiris and Isis, and all the other fables (of that kind), have reference to the stars, their configuration, their risings and settings.'

To early, nomadic man, the skies must, indeed, have seemed mysterious and all-powerful, and lore, gathered from their observations of the movements of the god-like stars, which marked the seasons of the year, was passed down through the generations. Both settled agriculture, which requires forward planning, and the human urge to discover what the gods have got in store, and to placate them, led to the formation of the calendar, and to the dawn of both astrology and astronomy, which remained one science until quite recent times.

Different cultures have found different gods and supernatural beings in the random pattern of the firmament of stars, which is thought by some to have given rise not only to the constellations as we know them, but also to the first alphabets. One image which most races share, however, is the great wheel of the zodiac – although the beasts themselves may vary – spinning on the still hub of the pole. This band of stars around the celestial equator, along which the sun and moon and all the planets move, was the 'twelve-spoked wheel' of the Indian 'Rig Veda', turning on the Pole Star, which was worshipped as the 'Pivot of the Planets'. As the zodiac is where the main celestial action is, it was the first part of the sky to be closely studied, and so to take on mythic forms which reflected the different seasons of the year. As time went by, records were made of the events on earth which coincided with the movements of the planets, and with the eclipses of the sun and moon. By around 700 BC in Babylon, a city ruled by omens, an announcement from an astro-specialist reads: 'This month a fox came into the city... this month's prices were... the moon was surrounded by a halo and within it were the Pleiades... reddish clouds were seen in the West... there was an earthquake on the 22nd, Mercury being 3½ ells behind the fish-tail in Capricorn.'

Astrology developed in complexity through the ages, reaching its zenith during the Renaissance, when Catherine de Medici had the visionary prophet, Nostradamus, as her advisor, and Elizabeth I had the mysterious Doctor Dee who, amongst other things, tried to found a telepathic secret service. The seeds of its decline were sown, however, when Copernicus discovered that the earth went round the sun, and it received its real death-blow in the early seventeenth century when Galileo, looking through his telescope, saw not angels but the rocks and craters of the moon. The Age of Reason, and of astronomy, had begun. For two centuries astrology was ignored, but since the end of the nineteenth century it has flowered once more.

But the zodiac, although important, accounts for only twelve of the constellations, which stretch from pole to pole, peopling the heavens with the contents of the human soul. Familiar to farmers, scholars, sailors and astronomers throughout the ages, the image of the heavens which these cards portray started to take form on the banks of the Tigris and the Euphrates as early, it is thought, as 5000 BC, but the civilisations of the Ganges and the Nile also played a part. Classical Greece altered some of the old myths, and overlaid them with its own, but the ancient Babylonian vision of the skies can often still be seen, disguised, behind the well-known Greek stories of later times.

The oldest description of the skies we have dates back to about 2000 BC, by which time forty-three of the forty-eight constellations, described by Ptolemy in the second century AD, were as we see them now. The early Arabians used the stars to guide them through the trackless desert wastes, just as the Mediterranean peoples did to find their way across the sea, but it is to the astronomers of eighth-century Baghdad, who kept the torch of learning alight during the European Dark Ages, and who were more interested in the stars themselves than in the constellations, that we owe many of the stars' exotic-sounding names.

After Ptolemy, few alterations were made to the heavens for 1300 years, until Ulug Beg, the grandson of the great Tamerlaine, published his new star 'Tables' in medieval Samarkand. Direct translations from the Greek, however, started to appear in Europe in the sixteenth and seventeenth centuries, when Copernicus and Galileo changed the way we see the world.

During the last hundred years, the visual images shown on these cards, and on the star charts of the past, have been banished from the skies to allow for greater accuracy and precision. It is to no less an artist than Dürer, who published two star maps in the sixteenth century, which were copied in one form or another in all the star atlases which came after, that we owe the Western vision of the constellations. Who created the older constellations, and why their shapes bear so little resemblance to the patterns of the actual stars, will, perhaps, always remain a mystery. In studying the lore surrounding the older ones, it must also be borne in mind that, thanks to the moving axis of the earth, which takes nearly 26,000 years to come full circle, the stars no longer rise and set at exactly the same time of year as they did in early times. Nor, sadly, are they any longer in alignment with the ancient temples which were built to celebrate them.

Although the Egyptian Pharaoh, Neku, is said to have sent a Phoenician fleet around the Horn of Africa in 600 BC, the southern skies were not charted until the advent of the Dutch explorers in the sixteenth century. Then, in 1603, the astronomer Johann Bayer filled the new stellar zone with the strange new birds and animals which the explorers had discovered, so that today, amongst others, a bird of paradise, a toucan, a phoenix, a flying fish, a chameleon and a crane now flock around the south celestial pole. In the 1750s, Nicolas La Caille, 'the true Columbus of the southern sky', added a selection of man-made tools, such as a compass, a chisel, a microscope, a builder's level, and the Table Mountain, at the Cape of Good Hope, from which he first surveyed the southern heavens. As these cards are designed for use primarily from the northern hemisphere, nineteen of these southern circumpolar constellations, which have no real mythical associations, are not included in the set. Forty-four of those included can, however, be seen from southern latitudes.

The cards themselves, originally hand-painted, were invented by 'a lady' and published in London in about 1825. Called *Urania's Mirror*, after the Greek muse of astronomy, they were and still are, an original and easy way to get to know the heavens.

HOW TO USE THE CARDS

The cards and the booklet are easy to use. Each card is pierced with holes of different sizes which mark the actual stars, large and small, in each constellation. They glitter when the card is held up to the light, so that you can learn to recognise the patterns of the constellations, and find them in the skies.

As the earth turns on its axis and makes its annual orbit of the sun, different stars become visible at different times of the year. Between pages 8-16 you will find descriptions of the night sky, by northern and southern season, from both hemispheres, and lists of which cards to use at which time of year. The stars listed for each season are those best seen at that time of year, although other constellations are often also visible.

Choose the biggest, brightest stars and constellations first, and familiarise yourself with two or three. The cards can be used out of doors with a torch – a red light will preserve your night vision – but it is best to get to know their unique patterns first in the comfort of your home.

The main part of the text, which lists the cards in order, contains more information about how to find each one. A constellation is often on view for several months, moving westwards through the sky. All instructions for locating stars assume the cards are used at approximately 10.30 p.m. local time (11.30 p.m. daylight saving time).

THE MAPS

The sky maps of the northern and southern hemispheres are there to help you place the constellations in relation to each other. If you want, you can also use them as a back-up to discover which ones are best seen at a particular time of year. Turn the map of the hemisphere you are in until the right month is at the bottom. You will then see which constellations are best seen when you face due south in the northern hemisphere between 10 and 11 p.m. local time, and when you face due north in the southern hemisphere. In the northern hemisphere for every hour earlier turn the map 15° in a clockwise direction. For every hour later turn it 15° in an anticlockwise direction. In the southern hemisphere, turn the map 15° anticlockwise for each hour earlier, and 15° clockwise for each hour later.

THE LETTERING
ON THE CARDS

On the cards, the brightest star in each constellation is marked by the first letter of the Greek alphabet, α, the second by β etc. After the twenty-four Greek letters have been used, small case Roman letters – a, b, c, etc. – are used, followed by capitals, A, B, C, etc. The spelling on the cards of star names sometimes differs from modern usage, which is occasionally used for clarity.

FROM THE
NORTHERN HEMISPHERE
THE CIRCUMPOLAR STARS

These constellations, which surround the North Celestial Pole, are *visible all year round* from average northern latitudes. URSA MAJOR, the Great Bear, which is also known as the PLOUGH and the BIG DIPPER, and the distinct, W-shaped CASSIOPEIA, are the brightest and easiest to recognise, so concentrate on finding these two before attempting to locate the others.

To find the POLE STAR, Polaris, which marks the tail of URSA MINOR, take a line from Merak, through Dubhe, the stars on URSA MAJOR's back, which are called the POINTERS, until you reach Polaris, which is situated at five times the distance between them.

Continuing clockwise around the pole from URSA MAJOR, we come to DRACO, the Dragon, and URSA MINOR. Next come CEPHEUS and CASSIOPEIA, which are almost opposite URSA MAJOR.

CAMELOPARDALIS and LYNX, two modern constellations, which are of little interest as they contain no bright stars, lie between CASSIOPEIA and URSA MAJOR, and complete the circle.

LACERTA, the Lizard, which lies to the side of CASSIOPEIA, and CANES VENATICI, the Hunting Dogs of BOÖTES, which are just south of URSA MAJOR's tail, are also counted as circumpolar stars.

☞ *THE CARDS TO USE* ☜

Camelopardalis · *Plate 2*   Draco & Ursa Minor · *Plate 1*
Canes Venatici · *Plate 10*   Lacerta · *Plate 14*
Cassiopeia · *Plate 3*   Lynx · *Plate 8*
Cepheus · *Plate 4*   Ursa Major · *Plate 9*

THE STARS IN WINTER

On winter evenings, the great constellation of ORION is in the south. Study the map of the northern hemisphere, and locate ORION. Once you have found it in the sky, you will be able to find Sirius in CANIS MAJOR, which follows at ORION's heels, Aldebaran in TAURUS, and Castor and Pollux in GEMINI. Capella in AURIGA is nearly overhead on the zenith. Above the eastern horizon lies Regulus, which marks the heart of LEO. The Great Bear, **URSA MAJOR**,* is in the northeast, and the 'great square of PEGASUS' is in the west. **CASSIOPEIA**, a clear, W-shaped constellation, is high up west of the zenith, and Vega, the Harp Star, in LYRA, is on the northern horizon. CETUS and ERIDANUS are in the southwest of the sky, the Milky Way spans the heavens from CYGNUS, through **CASSIOPEIA**, AURIGA, ORION and GEMINI down to the southern horizon. These are the major landmarks, and the other circumpolar stars are also on view (see previous section for cards to use for these), as are the smaller constellations in between them, which you will find on the map.

⟜ *THE CARDS TO USE* ⟜

Aries · *Plate 16*	Gemini · *Plate 18*
Andromeda · *Plate 5*	Leo · *Plate 20*
Auriga · *Plate 7*	Lyra, etc. · *Plate 14*
Canis Major, Lepus,	Orion · *Plate 29*
Columba · *Plate 30*	Perseus · *Plate 6*
Canis Minor &	Pegasus & Equuleus · *Plate 15*
Monoceros · *Plate 31*	Taurus · *Plate 17*
Eridanus & Cetus · *Plate 28*	

---

* Constellations in bold type are circumpolar constellations, mentioned in previous section.

THE STARS IN SPRING

Capella in AURIGA, Castor and Pollux in GEMINI and Procyon in CANIS MINOR are still quite high in the sky, although ORION is now setting in the west. W-shaped CASSIOPEIA is quite low in the northern sky, Vega in LYRA is in the east, but the season's brightest star is Arcturus (the fourth brightest star in the sky) in BOÖTES in the east. LEO is in the south, with CANCER and VIRGO on either side, and CORVUS, CRATER and HYDRA lie beneath them, nearer the southern horizon. Aldebaran in TAURUS is in the west. The circumpolar constellations, and some smaller groups, can also now be seen (see map).

☞ THE CARDS TO USE ☜

Auriga · *Plate 7*	Gemini · *Plate 18*
Boötes · *Plate 10*	Leo · *Plate 20*
Canis Minor · *Plate 31*	Lyra · *Plate 14*
Corvus, Crater,	Orion · *Plate 29*
Hydra · *Plate 32*	Taurus · *Plate 17*
Cancer · *Plate 19*	Virgo · *Plate 21*

THE STARS IN SUMMER

In the summer, the Harp Star, Vega in LYRA, is nearly overhead on the zenith next to HERCULES. Nearby lie CYGNUS and AQUILA. Deneb in CYGNUS, Athair in AQUILA (better known as Altair) and Vega in LYRA form the great 'Summer Triangle', which is easy to recognise in the northeast in the summer skies.

Capella in AURIGA is near the northern horizon and Arcturus in BOÖTES is in the west, as is the Great Bear, URSA MAJOR. In the east, the 'great square of PEGASUS' is rising, and on the southern horizon is Antares, the great red heart of SCORPIO. Above Antares is SERPENTARIUS (now known as Ophiuchus), and to the east is SAGITTARIUS. LIBRA and VIRGO lie to the west. Some smaller constellations can also now be seen (see map), as can most of the circumpolar constellations.

THE CARDS TO USE

Auriga · *Plate 7*	Libra · *Plate 22*
Boötes · *Plate 10*	Pegasus & Equuleus · *Plate 15*
Delphinus, Sagitta	Sagittarius · *Plate 24*
& Aquila · *Plate 13*	Scorpio · *Plate 23*
Hercules & Corona	Serpentarius (better known as
Borealis · *Plate 11*	Ophiuchus) · *Plate 12*
Lacerta, Cygnus, Lyra,	Virgo · *Plate 21*
Vulpecula · *Plate 14*	

THE STARS IN AUTUMN

The W-shaped constellation of CASSIOPEIA is nearly overhead on the zenith near ANDROMEDA and PERSEUS in the autumn, with CYGNUS and LYRA in the west and TAURUS in the east with AURIGA. Looking south, the 'great square of PEGASUS' glitters near the zenith, and the 'watery' constellations of CAPRICORNUS, AQUARIUS PISCIS AUSTRALIS, CETUS and ERIDANUS – the 'Sea' of ancient Babylon – can be seen nearer the horizon, with PISCES above them. Other, smaller constellations can now also be seen (see map), as can many of the circumpolar stars.

☞ THE CARDS TO USE ☜

Andromeda etc. · *Plate 5*

Aquarius & Piscis
  Australis · *Plate 26*

Aries · *Plate 16*

Auriga · *Plate 7*

Capricornus · *Plate 25*

Cetus & Eridanus · *Plate 28*

Cygnus & Lyra etc. · *Plate 14*

Pegasus & Equuleus · *Plate 15*

Pisces · *Plate 27*

Perseus · *Plate 6*

FROM THE
SOUTHERN HEMISPHERE

As these cards were designed primarily for use in the northern hemisphere, nineteen of the southern constellations which surround the South Celestial Pole and so cannot be seen from Europe, are not included. At least forty-four of the constellations on the cards, however, can be seen from southern latitudes – Australia and New Zealand. In these descriptions by (southern) season, I have only mentioned those included in the set. The southern circumpolar constellations can be located on the star map of the southern hemisphere.

THE STARS IN SUMMER

ORION is inverted high in the northeast, and Sirius in CANIS MAJOR is near the zenith overhead, with Procyon in CANIS MINOR nearby. The whole of ERIDANUS, including its main star, Achernar, which cannot be seen from northern latitudes, can be seen in the west, along with CETUS, the Sea Monster. Canopus (the second brightest star in the sky) in CARINA (the keel of the older ARGO NAVIS), is just east of the zenith. Aldebaran in TAURUS and Castor and Pollux in GEMINI can be seen above the northern horizon, with Capella in AURIGA below them.

☞ *THE CARDS TO USE* ☜

Andromeda · *Plate 5*	Cetus & Eridanus · *Plate 28*
Auriga · *Plate 7*	Gemini · *Plate 18*
Argo Navis &	Orion · *Plate 29*
Hydra, etc. · *Plate 32*	Taurus · *Plate 17*
Canis Major, etc. · *Plate 30*	
Canis Minor, etc. · *Plate 31*	

THE STARS IN AUTUMN

From LIBRA in the east, the zodiac band runs across the northern sky, through Spica in VIRGO and on through Regulus, the heart of LEO, to GEMINI in the northwest. ORION is higher in the west. Both Sirius in CANIS MAJOR and Procyon in CANIS MINOR lie west of the zenith overhead. Looking south, Canopus in CARINA (the keel of ARGO NAVIS) can be seen, as can the whole of ARGO NAVIS and CENTAURUS, which dominate the sky. Other, less important constellations can now also be seen (see map), including the nineteen southern circumpolar stars which are not included in the set.

THE CARDS TO USE	
Argo Navis &	Gemini · *Plate 28*
Centaurus · *Plate 32*	Libra · *Plate 22*
Cancer · *Plate 19*	Leo · *Plate 20*
Canis Major, etc. · *Plate 30*	Orion · *Plate 29*
Canis Minor, etc. · *Plate 31*	Virgo · *Plate 21*

THE STARS IN WINTER

L ooking north, Arcturus in BOÖTES can be seen with Vega, the Harp Star in LYRA, next to HERCULES low on the horizon. Above it lies SERPENTARIUS (marked on the map as OPHIUCHUS) grappling with the SERPENS, the Serpent, with Athair (better known as Altair) in AQUILA in the east. Antares in SCORPIO shines red near the zenith overhead, with Spica in VIRGO to the west of it. SAGITTARIUS and CAPRICORNUS are in the east, and CENTAURUS, CORVUS, CRATER and HYDRA are together in the west. Other smaller groups of stars can also be seen (see map), including the southern circumpolar constellations.

☞ *THE CARDS TO USE* ☜

Aquila, etc · *Plate 13*	Lyra · *Plate 14*
Boötes · *Plate 10*	Virgo · *Plate 21*
Capricornus · *Plate 25*	Sagittarius · *Plate 24*
Centaurus, Corvus,	Scorpio · *Plate 23*
Crater, Hydra · *Plate 32*	Serpentarius (best known
Hercules · *Plate 11*	as Ophiuchus) &
Libra · *Plate 22*	Serpens · *Plate 12*

THE STARS IN SPRING

The ancient Babylonian 'Sea', containing CAPRICORN, AQUARIUS, PISCIS AUSTRALIS and CETUS, the Sea Monster, fills much of the northern sky, with the 'great square of PEGASUS' in the centre and Athair (better known as Altair) in AQUILA in the west. ORION is rising in the east, Fomalhaut in PISCIS AUSTRALIS is near the zenith, and Achernar, the end of the River ERIDANUS, lies in the centre of the southern sky. Other, smaller groups can also now be seen, including the southern circumpolar constellations.

☞ *THE CARDS TO USE* ☜

Aquila, etc · *Plate 13*
Aquarius & Piscis
   Australis · *Plate 26*
Aries · *Plate 16*
Capricornus · *Plate 25*

Cetus & Eridanus · *Plate 28*
Orion · *Plate 29*
Pegasus & Equuleus · *Plate 15*
Pisces · *Plate 27*

THE
PLATES

17

```
┌─────────────────────────────────────┐
│                                       │
│            ██ PLATE 1 ██               │
│                                       │
│              D R A C O                 │
│           the DRAGON and               │
│         U R S A   M I N O R            │
│          the LITTLE BEAR               │
│                                       │
└─────────────────────────────────────┘
```

DRACO · THE DRAGON

The dragon, which was well known for its vigilance and sharp vision, was the traditional guardian of temples and treasures, and of the springs of life and immortality in the ancient world.

Here, it coils around the North Celestial Pole, guarding the 'still point in the turning world' which, like the empty centre of the Hindu Wheel of Transformations, and the hole in the middle of the jade disc which the Chinese used to symbolise the heavens, was the 'Unmoved Mover', both the cause and destination of all life. The celestial pole is thus symbolic of a 'hole' in the space-time continuum, the doorway between time and eternity, guarded by the dragon, the Dweller on the Threshold, which the hero, Hercules (see plate 11), crushes underfoot, triumphing over death and darkness.

In the myth of Hercules, Draco, our Dragon, 'ever vigilant because it never sets', is Ladon, the guardian of the golden apples of immortality which grew in the garden of the Hesperides, beyond Oceanus, the River of Time, in the far west, which is the land of death. Like Ladon, which is also the name of the river which snaked around the magical garden, Oceanus is both serpent and river, encircling the world with the zodiac on his back, and dividing time from eternity. (See Hercules).

URSA MINOR · THE LITTLE BEAR

Although the Little Bear is famous as the home of the Pole Star, it was, in fact, invented in the sixth century BC as a guide for sailors. It has no real myths attached to it, and was created from the Dragon's wing, now long forgotten, which it replaced.

The Stars

Because of the precession of the equinoxes, the North Celestial Pole appears to change in relation to its stellar background, taking nearly 26,000 years to come full circle. As a result, several stars have been the Pole Star, the closest to 'true North', during recorded history.

In 10,000 BC, Vega, the Harp Star in Lyra, marked the pole. By around 3000 BC it was Thuban, the main star in the Dragon. As it lies halfway down its body, the entire constellation appeared to swing round it, as on a pivot, like the hands of a clock in reverse motion, echoing once more its connection with time and eternity. It could be seen by both day and night from the bottom of the main, central passage of the great pyramid of Cheops at Ghizeh. (The stars can, in fact, be seen in broad daylight from the bottom of any deep well.)

The orange star, Kochab, which marks the back of the Little Bear, is now known as the Guardian of the Pole, and was the Pole Star around 1000 BC.

Polaris, our present Pole Star, will be at its closest to 'true North' in AD 2095.

The stars of the Little Bear, which once marked the Dragon's wing, are known as the Seven Sleepers of Ephesus, who dreamt on in their Turkish grotto, undisturbed, for 200 years.

To Locate

Merak and Dubhe (plate 9), which mark the end of the Plough, are known as the Pointers, as a line continued through them points to Polaris, the Pole Star.

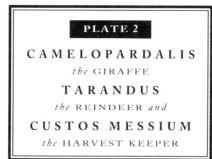

PLATE 2

CAMELOPARDALIS
the GIRAFFE

TARANDUS
the REINDEER *and*

CUSTOS MESSIUM
the HARVEST KEEPER

CAMELOPARDALIS · THE GIRAFFE

Camelopardalis, the Giraffe, behind whose neck lies the Pole Star, was created by the astronomer, Bartschius, in 1614. It has no bright stars.

TARANDUS · THE REINDEER

Now no longer in the heavens, it was invented by Le Monnier in 1736 to commemorate his trip to Lapland.

CUSTOS MESSIUM · THE HARVEST KEEPER

The astronomer, Lalande, created Custos Messium in 1775, and called it Le Messier, after his friend, who was known as the 'comet ferret' by Louis XV of France: he was the 'keeper' of the 'harvest' of comets, twelve of which he discovered in four years. Lalande, who passed whole nights on the Pont Neuf in Paris, accosting passers-by and explaining astronomy to anyone who would listen, spent the French Revolution in his observatory and 'thanked his stars' for saving him from the guillotine. It is no longer marked on star charts.

To Locate

These are northern circumpolar constellations. See map.

PLATE 3

CASSIOPEIA

Cassiopeia, the legendary Ethiopian queen, seated on her throne, was the mother of Andromeda (plate 5) and the wife of Cepheus (plate 4; see also Perseus, plate 6). She boasted that she was more beautiful than all the sea nymphs and is now doomed, as punishment, to circle the pole for ever, upside down. As an Ethiopian, she has sometimes been known as a black queen. Arab astronomers called this constellation the Large Hand Stained with Henna, and to the Celts it was the home of the god Don, who was later thought of as the King of the Fairies and who ruled the Milky Way, where this constellation lies.

The Stars

Its pale rose leading star, Schedir, marks the queen's breast. Near Chaph, on the throne, a famous 'nova' suddenly appeared in 1572. So bright it could be seen in broad daylight, it became known as 'The Stranger', and was thought to be the reappearance of the Star of Bethlehem, heralding Christ's second coming. It is now called Tycho's Star after the astronomer Tycho Brahé, whose faith in astrology was so great that in his catalogue of the heavens he reduced the number of stars to the mystical number of 777.

To Locate

Cassiopeia, an easily recognisable W-shaped constellation lying between her daughter, Andromeda, and the North Celestial Pole, is on view all year round from average northern latitudes. See the descriptions of the sky, by season, to know exactly where to look. It cannot be seen from the southern hemisphere.

PLATE 4

CEPHEUS

Cepheus, the King of 'Ethiopia', was the father of Andromeda and the husband of Cassiopeia (see Perseus, plate 6). Not much is known about him, except that he accompanied the Argonauts on their quest for the Golden Fleece, and now sits with his left foot on the pole. He is, however, of Chaldean origin, and was the son of Belos, the mythical inventor of astronomy. In prehistoric India, he was Kapi, the Ape-god, and two of his stars, in 21000 BC and in 19000 BC, respectively, marked the North Celestial Pole. In China these stars were known as the 'Inner Throne of the Five Emperors'.

The Stars

Alderamin, which marks the king's right shoulder, will be the Pole Star in AD 7500.

To Locate

Cepheus lies between his wife, Cassiopeia, and the Dragon, and is circumpolar in the northern hemisphere, and so on view all year. It cannot be seen from the southern hemisphere.

PLATE 5

GLORIA
FREDERICI,
ANDROMEDA
and
TRIANGULA

GLORIA FREDERICI

It is now no longer a constellation. Created in 1787 in honour of Frederick II of Prussia, its inventor moved Andromeda's right hand into the position shown on the card in order to make room for it, little caring that her hand had 'stretched out there for 3000 years'.

ANDROMEDA

Andromeda, the archetypal damsel in distress, forever chained in space and waiting to be devoured by Cetus, the sea monster, was the daughter of Cepheus and Cassiopeia, the legendary King and Queen of Ethiopia. (See Perseus, plate 6.) The origins of the entire 'Ethiopian' royal family, in fact, go back to the great Babylonian 'Epic of Creation', as do Perseus and the sea monster, which was the Dragon of Chaos overcome by the hero Bel Marduk.

The Stars

Sirrah, better known as Alpherat, Andromeda's most important star, lies just by her left ear. It brought honour and riches to those born under its influence. It is at its height on 10 November in the northern hemisphere. In the centre of the constellation lies the famous Andromeda galaxy. Seen through the veil of our own galaxy, the Milky Way, which is less than 5000 light years distant, the Andromeda galaxy, more than two million light years away, is the most distant object in the universe visible to the naked eye and is thought to be very similar in shape to the Milky Way.

To Locate

Andromeda is visible from August to January in the northern hemisphere, and in November south of the equator. It lies between Pisces and Cassiopeia (see map). The Andromeda galaxy can be found by following a line of two stars from Mirach, Andromeda's second star, which marks her lap.

TRIANGULA

Now called Triangulum, it was known to the Greeks as Deltatron, because its shape resembled the Greek letter, delta. The Romans, however, saw it as the island of Sicily in the sky, which Ceres, the harvest goddess, had begged Jove to re-create in the heavens. It has also been identified with Thrinakia in Homer's *Odyssey*, the pasture of the Oxen of the Sun.

The Stars

Close to its main star, a spiral galaxy the size of a full moon can just be made out.

To Locate

It lies just south of Andromeda on the borders of the Milky Way.

PLATE 6

PERSEUS

and the

CAPUT MEDUSAE,

the GORGON'S HEAD

Between Cassiopeia, the boastful Ethiopian queen who claimed she was more beautiful than the sea nymphs, and her daughter, Andromeda, chained to a rock as a punishment for her mother's pride, lies Perseus, her rescuer, and one of the greatest of the Greek heroes, holding the Gorgon's head.

Perseus' conception marks him as a hero from the start. His mother Danaë, was imprisoned by her father in a subterranean chamber, but Zeus desired her, and rained down on her as a shower of gold. Perseus' quest was to kill the snake-haired gorgon, Medusa, whose gaze turned men to stone. Armed with a polished shield given to him by the gods, so that he did not have to look evil in the face when he chopped off Medusa's head, he journeyed to the Gorgon's lair in the far west of the world. His feat accomplished, Perseus mounted the winged horse, Pegasus, which had sprung from the blood of Medusa's severed neck. Flying through the Aegean skies on him, carrying the gruesome head, he saw Andromeda chained to a rock, about to be devoured by a sea monster. One glance from the Gorgon's head, however, turned it to stone.

The Stars

In early August, when Perseus first starts to rise low in the northern sky, the earth passes through a comet's tail, resulting in our richest annual rain of shooting stars. Because they appear to stream towards us from his constellation, they are known as the

Perseids, after the house of heroes which he founded, to which Hercules also belonged. This shower of meteors, which coincides with the annual rising of the constellation, could explain how the story of Perseus' conception by a shower of gold began. To the side of Perseus lies Algol, or Ras-al-Ghul, the ghoul's head, which marks the notorious Medusa's head. Algol has always been referred to as the 'Demon Star', the most malefic in the heavens. Every three days, for a short while, its light dims and then grows slowly brighter, which may have reminded the ancient Greek astronomers of the Gorgon's baleful, petrifying stare. It is, in fact, the brightest of the 'eclipsing binaries', twin stars which revolve endlessly around each other, and temporarily obscure each other's light.

To Locate

Turn towards the north during late summer and autumn, take a line from the Pole Star to Cassiopeia, and on down to Algenib, Perseus' leading star, which marks one of the ribs of the hero's Y-shaped constellation. Perseus hardly rises above the horizon in the southern hemisphere.

Auriga, the charioteer who, mysteriously, lost his chariot long ago, stretches across the Milky Way with his Goat and Kids, between Taurus and Camelopardalis.

The connection between the celestial charioteer and Capella, the Little She-Goat, is also shrouded in mystery, but they appear to have been together in the skies for at least 5000 years.

The Charioteer himself is thought to be Erechthonious, the deformed son of the earth, and the lame god, Vulcan. He was raised by Athene, goddess of wisdom, who placed the infant in a box, which she then gave into the care of two maidens, forbidding them to open it. They disobeyed, but when they saw the child inside, entwined by a serpent, they fled in terror and fell to their death from the Acropolis in Athens.

Erechthonious became the King of Athens and invented the four-horse chariot, for which he was placed in the heavens by the gods.

Four horses also draw the sun's chariot, which Phaeton drove, burning the earth by allowing the horses to gallop out of control through the skies.

The Stars

Capella, the Little She-Goat, or the Goat Star, is the sixth brightest in the sky. It was the Patron Star of Babylon. In India, it is the heart of Brahma and, to the Arabs, it is the overseer of the celestial game in which the other stars are the players. In Egypt, around 5000 BC, temples were built in alignment with its setting, and to the Greeks it was the she-goat, Amalthea, who suckled the infant Zeus, perhaps because it is located in the Milky Way.

To Locate

The main stars of Auriga form a large pentagon, which lies north of Taurus and between Perseus and Gemini (see map of the northern hemisphere). It is almost circumpolar and so on view most of the year in the northern hemisphere. It is overhead at 10 p.m. in early January. (See pages for descriptions of the sky by season.)

Capella can be seen low on the northern horizon in January in the southern hemisphere.

LYNX

The Lynx is a modern constellation, invented in the late seventeenth century by the astronomer, Hevelius, who claimed that you had to be lynx-eyed to see it, as it contains no bright stars, although it does cover a large area.

To Locate

See the description of the northern circumpolar stars on page 8.

TELESCOPIUM HERSCHILII

Created by the Abbé Hell in 1781, in honour of the famous astronomer, Sir William Herschel, it is no longer listed as a constellation.

PLATE 9

URSA MAJOR
the GREAT BEAR

In ancient Greece and Babylon, in India and in North America in early times, Ursa Major, the best-known constellation in the northern sky, has been seen as a she-bear. It is also known as the Big Dipper and the Plough.

The Bear was first placed in the Greek skies by Zeus, who loved the nymph, Callisto, one of the chaste maidens of Artemis, the virgin goddess of the chase. To save Callisto and her unborn baby from the Virgin's wrath, Zeus turned her into the Great Bear and placed her by the pole. Arctos, the Bear and Arcturus (Boötes) her son, the Bear Keeper, gave their names to the Arctic wastes. Because the constellation circles round the still point of the pole, which is the 'axis' of the world, it was the Sanskrit Driver of the Axle, whom the Greeks turned into Ixion, spinning for ever on the flaming wheel of the zodiac and the constellations (see Sagittarius). In early England it was King Arthur's chariot and his home. Arth means 'bear', and Uthyr 'wonderful', and the origin of the Round Table, with the Holy Grail in the centre, may be similar to that of Ixion's spinning wheel (see Draco for the symbolism of the north pole). Later, it was traditionally called Charles's Wain, or Wagon, thanks to the legendary association between King Arthur and the Emperor Charlemagne, who both had courts of chivalrous knights and who both, it is said, are not dead but sleeping, ready to awaken and save their countries in their hour of need. As the Plough, perhaps its best-known name, it has been traced back to prehistoric India, where it was the ox-drawn plough, invented by Boötes, which he drives around the pole. In the south of France it is the Casserole.

The Stars

The names of the seven most important stars in the Great Bear are Dubhe, Merak, Phachd, Megrez, Alioth, Mizar and Benetnasch. Dubhe: 'Bear', and Merak: 'Loin', are known as the Pointers, as a line taken through them points at the Pole Star. The Great Bear points the way to several other constellations, and is one that everyone can recognise. (See descriptions of the northern sky, by season, on pp. 8-12 and map, to locate.) Very close to Mizar, on the tail, lies Alcor, which has probably grown brighter during the last thousand years. They were traditionally used as an eyesight test for armies, although now it is much easier than it used to be to distinguish between them.

PLATE 10

BOÖTES
the HERDSMAN
CANES VENATICI
the HUNTING DOGS
COMA BERENICES
BERENICE'S HAIR *and*
QUADRANS
MURALIS

BOÖTES · THE HERDSMAN

Boötes, the celestial Herdsman, was also the mythical inventor of the ox-drawn plough, and as such, perhaps, immortalises the transition from a nomadic life to settled agriculture in the ancient world. More importantly, he is connected with the two Bears, which he herds – or chases – around the northern pole.

Zeus fell in love with Callisto, one of the nymphs of Artemis, the chaste goddess of the hunt. When she discovered that Callisto was pregnant, Artemis attempted to destroy her, but Zeus turned Callisto into a bear and placed her in the skies as Ursa Major, the Great Bear. Arcas, their son, is Boötes, the Bear Keeper.

The Stars

Arcturus, which is about thirty-five light years distant and marks Boötes' knee, is the brightest star in the northern hemisphere, and the fourth brightest in the sky. Its name means Bear Keeper in Greek, and it was greatly feared by sailors, as it presaged stormy weather, although astrologically it brought honour and riches. To the Arab astronomers it was the Keeper of Heaven. Nekkar, which marks Boötes' ear, is the Herdsman.

CANES VENATICI · THE HUNTING DOGS

Held on a leash by Boötes, these two greyhounds, which were invented in 1690, pursue the Great Bear around the North Pole. Their names are Asterion, the Starry, and Chara, Dear to the Heart of her Master.

The Stars

Cor Caroli, or Charles's Heart, is seen as a heart with a crown on Chara's collar. It was named in memory of Charles II, as it is said to have shone with especial brilliance when he returned to England from exile on 29 May, 1660, to ascend the throne.

COMA BERENICES · BERENICE'S HAIR

Berenice's Hair, the beautiful amber-coloured tresses of Queen Berenice of Egypt, became a constellation around 243 BC. When Queen Berenice's husband, Ptolemy Euergetes, set off to fight the Assyrians, she vowed to sacrifice her hair in gratitude for his safe return. She kept her word, and placed her severed tresses in the temple of Venus, whence they were stolen and placed in the skies. Some say Venus herself was the thief, others that the astronomer, who invented the constellation, made up the story to console Berenice for the loss. To Chaucer, it was Berenice's Bush. At least a thousand galaxies, too distant to be seen, hide behind her hair.

To Locate

All these stars can be seen in spring and summer in the northern hemisphere between the Great Bear to the north, and Virgo to the south. They are hardly visible at all from the southern hemisphere, but Arcturus can be seen on the northern horizon in June. Quadrans Muralis is no longer a constellation, and Coma Berenices has no bright stars.

PLATE 11

HERCULES
and
CORONA BOREALIS
the NORTHERN CROWN

HERCULES

Known to the early Greeks as the Kneeling One, or as the Phantom, whose foot rests on the head of the Dragon which guards the north pole, this mysterious figure later became the great hero, Hercules, whose name, perhaps, means 'glory of the air'. Wearing the lion skin which made him invincible, he is seen threatening Cerberus, the hound of hell, with his club.

Hercules undertook his famous 'labours' as a penance for killing his own children in a fit of madness. They are:

1   He kills the Nemean Lion, which had been ravaging the countryside, and dons its skin.

2   He overcomes the famous many-headed Hydra.

3   He captures alive the savage boar of Erymanthus.

4   He kills the Stymphalian Birds, whose wings of iron blotted out the sun, with a rain of arrows.

5   He chases the Ceryneian Hind, who had golden antlers and hoofs of bronze, for a whole year and brings her back alive.

6   He cleans out the Augean stables, which 3,000 oxen had lived in for thirty years, in one day.

7   He captures the mad bull of King Minos of Crete.

8   He captures and tames the wild, flesh-eating mares of Diomedes.

9   He kills the Queen of the Amazons and wins her girdle.

10   He kills the three-headed herdsman, and his two-headed dog, who guarded the red oxen of Geryon.

11   He kills the dragon, Ladon, who guarded the golden apples of the Hesperides (see Draco), and takes the apples, a symbol of immortality.

12   After initiating himself into the mysteries of the underworld, he goes down to capture Cerberus, the hound of hell who guards the gates of death, and strangles him with his bare hands.

For three years he was also the servant of Omphale, the Queen of Lydia, whose name means the 'navel of the world', and whose lover he became. He spent his time there wearing women's clothes and jewellery, and spinning yarn, which may be a reference to the early fertility rites of the Great Mother goddess and her subordinate son-lover.

At his death, no sooner had the flames been lit around his funeral pyre than a cloud came down, and in a flash of thunder and lightning he vanished from men's eyes and joined the gods.

Lions have always been associated with the sun, and so the lion skin marks Hercules as a solar hero; his Twelve Labours, ending in the winning of the golden apples of immortality and the conquest of death, have been compared to the sun's annual passage through the zodiac and to the journey of the soul of man.

He was, perhaps, originally the Euphratian hero, Gilgamesh, who conquered Tiamat, the great dragon of chaos.

The Stars

The entire solar system is moving towards Hercules, upon whose hip, in the deep sky, a 'globular cluster' of 100,000 stars can just be made out with the naked eye.

To Locate

Hercules is best seen in summer. He lies upside down between Draco and Ophiuchus, with his foot on the Dragon's head, and is bordered by Lyra to the east and by Corona Borealis to the west. In the southern hemisphere, where the Hero is on view the right way up, he can be seen from May to August.

CORONA BOREALIS · THE NORTHERN CROWN

Upside down behind the back of Hercules lies the Northern Crown, which belonged to Ariadne, the daughter of King Minos of Crete, whose ball of thread helped Theseus to defeat the Minotaur. Some say this is the jewelled crown which Theseus gave her on their marriage, before he abandoned her on the Greek island of Naxos. Others that it was the crown given to Ariadne by Bacchus, whom she then married. To the Celts, it was Caer (or Castle of) Arianrhod, the daughter of Don, King of the Fairies and, according to Robert Graves, the place where the souls of kings, poets and magicians went after death.

The Stars

In the centre of the arc of seven stars, which makes up the crown, lies Gemma, the central 'gem' in the crown. Corona Borealis contains a cluster of 400 galaxies, lying a thousand million light years away, which is invisible to the naked eye.

```
┌─────────────────────────────────────┐
│  ┌───────────────────────────────┐  │
│  │                               │  │
│  │        ███████████████        │  │
│  │        PLATE 12               │  │
│  │                               │  │
│  │         T A U R U S           │  │
│  │   P O N I A T O W S K I ,     │  │
│  │   S E R P E N T A R I U S     │  │
│  │       the HEALER              │  │
│  │   S C U T U M   S O B I E S K Y │ │
│  │      the SHIELD and           │  │
│  │        S E R P E N S          │  │
│  │       the SERPENT             │  │
│  │                               │  │
│  └───────────────────────────────┘  │
└─────────────────────────────────────┘
```

SERPENTARIUS · THE HEALER
SERPENS · THE SERPENT

Between the wild Archer, Sagittarius, and Boötes, the keeper of the Bears, Serpentarius, now known as Ophiuchus, wrestles with the Serpent, with his foot on the heart of the Scorpion he defeated.

Serpentarius is the Greek god of medicine, Asclepius, who learned the Healing Arts from the noble centaur, Chiron, in the forest glades of Greece, holding the serpent which remains the symbol of western medicine to this day.

After fasting and bathing, the sick and disturbed would spend the night in special 'dream incubation chambers' in his temples. The god, appearing to them in vivid dreams, diagnosed disease and offered cures, and the grateful recipients of his wisdom would then throw golden coins into his sacred fountains. His daughters were Hygieia, health, and Panacea, cure.

Rescued at birth from his mother's funeral pyre by his father, Apollo, who gave him to the centaur, Chiron, to bring up, Asclepius soon learned from him the secrets of all medicines and herbs. (See Centaurus, plate 32.) With the help of some of the

Gorgon's blood, given to him by Athene, the goddess of wisdom, and an unnamed plant, whose properties were revealed to him by a serpent, he even succeeded in resurrecting the dead. He tried to save Orion, the great hunter, from his death from a scorpion's sting, but the king of the underworld was angry that the laws of destiny and of nature were being broken, and so to pacify him Zeus killed Asclepius with a thunderbolt and placed him in the skies.

The snake is a homeopathic symbol of the poison which can both kill and cure and, because the creature sheds its skin, it represents rebirth. Here, Asclepius wrestles with it and controls it, transforming its poison and evil into wisdom and healing.

Part of Serpentarius lies between Scorpius and Sagittarius, and so is thought by some modern astrologers to be a thirteenth zodiac sign.

The Stars

The main star in this constellation, now known as Ophiuchus, from the Greek ophis (serpent), is called Ras Alhague, Head of the Serpent Charmer. Far more famous is Barnard's Star, a red dwarf not visible to the naked eye and the fourth closest to our sun. It is thought to have planets around it, which could be the home of life, and appears to us to be the fastest-moving star in space.

Serpens has now been divided into Serpens Caput, the Serpent's Head and Serpens Cauda, the Serpent's Tail.

SCUTUM SOBIESKY · THE SHIELD

The shield is a small constellation showing the coat of arms, emblazoned with the Christian cross, of the third John Sobiesky, King of Poland. It was invented by the astronomer Hevelius to commemorate King John's victory in 1683, when he repulsed the Turks from Vienna.

TAURUS PONIATOWSKI

Poniatowski's Bull was named after Stanislaus Poniatowski, King of Poland in 1777, by a Polish abbot who wanted to honour his king. The V-shaped pattern of its stars reminded him of the Hyades, which make up the face of Taurus.

To Locate

Serpentarius is a large, roundish constellation, almost empty of stars in the middle, which lies south of Hercules and partly between Scorpio and Sagittarius on the zodiac band. All these constellations are best seen in summer in the northern hemisphere, and winter in the southern.

PLATE 13

DELPHINUS
the DOLPHIN

SAGITTA
the ARROW

AQUILA
the EAGLE *and*

ANTINOUS

DELPHINUS · THE DOLPHIN

The swiftest and most intelligent of marine animals, the dolphin, is immortalised in the heavens as the Friend of Man.

Arion, a legendary poet and musician, was sailing back to Greece when the ship's crew turned against him, but with his lyre he summoned up a school of dolphins, who are notorious for their love of music. Throwing himself on their mercy, he jumped into the sea and was carried to safety by the dolphin who now shines among the stars. When they reached their destination, the dolphin insisted on accompanying Arion to the court, where it rapidly succumbed to a life of luxury.

It is also the dolphin who helped Poseidon to find the mermaid, Amphitrite, and who brought her back to be the sea god's queen in his golden palace at the bottom of the sea. As a reward, it was placed in the skies. The dolphin is a symbol of philanthropy and was known by the Greeks as the Sacred Fish.

SAGITTA · THE ARROW

Flying between Cygnus, the Swan, and Aquila, the Eagle, is the Arrow – the third smallest constellation in the sky. The emblem of both Apollo and Diana, it symbolises supreme power. This one is said to have been shot by Hercules at the dreaded

Stymphalian birds, who had claws, beaks and wings of iron, and who lived on human flesh in the marshes of Arcadia. It is also the arrow which killed Jupiter's eagle, and Cupid's love-dealing dart.

AQUILA · THE EAGLE

From Europe to the Far East, the eagle is the bird connected with the gods of war and power. It is the messenger from heaven, leading souls to immortality. This is the 'storm bird' of Zeus, who abducted the beautiful youth, Ganymede, and carried him through the air to Mount Olympus to be the cup-bearer of the gods. To ancient astronomers, Ganymede was Aquarius, the Water Carrier, who lies to the east nearby. Aquila has been recognised as a bird for at least 3500 years.

ANTINOUS

Underneath the eagle kneels Antinous, the favourite of the Roman Emperor Hadrian, who was immortalised in AD 132. An oracle revealed that the only thing which could prolong the ailing Emperor's life was the sacrifice of the object he most loved, and so Antinous willingly drowned himself in the waters of the Nile. After his death, Hadrian's courtiers pointed out to him the soul of Antinous shining in the sky. It is now no longer listed amongst the constellations.

To Locate

None of the stars in these constellations were large or bright enough to gather individual myths around them, but the flattened diamond shape of Delphinus, sometimes known as Job's Coffin, is easy to recognise. It is best seen in late summer in the northern hemisphere. The whole group lies west of Aquarius, in a rich part of the Milky Way. (Together, Vega in

Lyra, Deneb in Cygnus and Athair – better known as Altair – in Aquila make up the great 'Summer Triangle' in the northern skies.) From the southern hemisphere, they are in the centre of the northern sky from July to October. (See p.15-16 and map.)

PLATE 14

LACERTA
the LIZARD
CYGNUS
the SWAN
LYRA
the LYRE
VULPECULA *and*
ANSER
the FOX *and* GOOSE

LACERTA · THE LIZARD

Lacerta, the lizard was invented by the astronomer Hevelius in the seventeenth century. To the Chinese it was a flying dragon.

CYGNUS · THE SWAN

Like the lyre, with which Orpheus overcame the infernal powers, the Swan, with which it is often associated, is connected with music and death. Even though no one has ever heard its mythical 'swan song', with which it celebrates its longing for paradise just before it dies, the legend lives on, just as Cygnus, the great white Swan, continues to fly, with wings outstretched, southwards down the Milky Way.

Cygnus started out in life as a Trojan hero who was killed by Achilles and transformed, at the last moment, into a white swan by his father, the sea god Poseidon. When Achilles stripped him of his armour, he was gone. This is also the swan which Zeus changed into to seduce Leda. The product of their union was two enormous eggs, from which sprang Castor and Pollux, the Heavenly Twins – immortalised in the zodiac sign of Gemini – and Clytemnestra and Helen of Troy, 'the face that launched a thousand ships, and sank the topless towers of Illium'.

Zeus also tricked Nemesis, the stern goddess of Fate, and seduced her in the form of a white swan when she took pity on the Eagle, Aquila, which the Swan pursues through all eternity along the Milky Way.

The Stars

The brightest stars in Cygnus, form the 'Northern Cross'. Deneb, its brightest star, marks its tail, and Albireo, its beak.

LYRA · THE LYRE

The lyre was created by Mercury from a tortoiseshell. He gave it to Apollo, god of music and prophecy, who placed it in the heavens. Primitive music often imitates the rhythm and the movements of wild animals and birds, which throws light on the story of Orpheus, whose lyre this is. Orpheus, 'the singer whose song has power to tame all creatures, to gather wild animals and trees around him, who moves stones and cliffs, and even overcomes the laws of Hades', married the wood nymph Eurydice, but she died soon after from a serpent's bite. Overcome by grief, Orpheus entered the land of the dead and charmed the sovereigns of the underworld with the music of his lyre. Even the Furies wept at the sound of his music and Eurydice was allowed to return to the land of the living as long as Orpheus did not look round to see if she was following him. He did not trust the Queen of Hell sufficiently, however, and as he turned to make quite sure, Eurydice faded back once more into the underworld.

He also helped the Argonauts in their quest for the golden fleece, by playing while the ship sailed past the singing sirens.

Orpheus died a grisly death at the hands of a band of jealous women, who tore him limb from limb when he ignored them, and his head, and lyre, were washed out to sea from Asia Minor to the isle of Lesbos in the Aegean. His lyre was placed in a temple there, and his head, lodged between the rocks, gave oracles.

He is known as the Bringer of Culture and the Father of Mysticism, and because of his violent death, his descent into the underworld, and the school of mysteries which he founded, he has been compared with Christ.

The Stars

In 10,000 BC Vega, the legendary Harp Star, marked the North Celestial Pole, and was the centre of the ancient heavens. Some of the earliest Mesopotamian and Egyptian temples are said to have been built in alignment with it but, because of the precession of the equinoxes, it is no longer the 'still point in the turning world'. Along with Deneb in the Swan, and Altair in the Eagle, it forms part of the great 'summer triangle', the brightest stars in the northern summer skies.

VULPECULA AND ANSER · THE FOX AND GOOSE

The little Fox and Goose were also created by Hevelius but the Goose is no longer on modern star charts.

To Locate

Cygnus and Lyra, the Swan and the Lyre, are best seen between June and October in the northern hemisphere. They are at their highest point in September, when Cygnus is almost overhead on the zenith. From the southern hemisphere, Cygnus can be seen on the northern horizon in September, and Vega, in June.

PLATE 15

PEGASUS
the WINGED HORSE *and*
EQUULEUS
the FOAL

PEGASUS

Pegasus was the son of the great sea god, Neptune, and the Gorgon Medusa. When Perseus cut off Medusa's head, Pegasus, whose name means the 'Springs of Ocean' was born, according to one version of the story, from the blood which fell into the sea. The Gorgon's blood was also thought to be the origin of coral.

Snowy white with a mane of gold, Pegasus was the favourite of the Muses as his hoof marks caused their fountain of inspiration to start flowing. Bellerephon found him one day drinking at his fountain and tried to ride him up to heaven, but an insect's sting, delivered at the gods' command, caused the horse to throw his rider, who 'fell headlong through the fields of air'. Alone, Pegasus soared up to heaven, where he became the Thundering Horse of Jove and the carrier of the divine lightning.

The Stars

The 'Great Square of Pegasus' dominates the autumn sky and its main star, Markab, the Saddle, marks his shoulder.

EQUULEUS · THE FOAL

Behind Pegasus lies the Foal, which was thought by some to be Celeris, the Swift, the brother of Pegasus which Mercury, the ruler of the Zodiac sign, Gemini, gave to the famous horseman Castor, who was Pollux's mortal twin.

The Stars

The Foal is the second smallest constellation in the sky.

To Locate

Looking towards the south between August and December, or towards the north from the southern hemisphere in spring, it is hard to miss the 'Great Square'. Cassiopeia, Pisces and Andromeda, which surround it, can easily be found once it has been recognised.

```
┌─────────────────────────────────────┐
│  ┌─────────────────────────────────┐  │
│  │                                 │  │
│  │          ▇▇▇▇▇▇▇▇▇▇▇            │  │
│  │           PLATE 16              │  │
│  │                                 │  │
│  │           A R I E S             │  │
│  │          the RAM and            │  │
│  │                                 │  │
│  │    MUSCA  BOREALIS              │  │
│  │     the FLY OF THE NORTH        │  │
│  │                                 │  │
│  └─────────────────────────────────┘  │
└─────────────────────────────────────┘
```

ARIES · THE RAM

Aries, the Ram, is the first sign of the zodiac and is related to dawn, the spring, and the beginning of life.

THE ORIGIN OF THE GOLDEN FLEECE

When Mercury, the messenger of the gods, discovered that Phrixus and Helle, the children of the King of Thebes, were being badly treated by their stepmother Ino, he sent a supernatural ram, that could both speak and reason, to rescue them. Clinging to its fleece, they flew to Colchis, but Helle fell into the sea and gave her name to the Hellespont, near Istanbul, in which she drowned. On arrival, Phrixus sacrificed the ram and hung its fleece up in a sacred grove, where it was turned to gold. The story of Jason and the Argonauts and their quest for the Golden Fleece, is told under Argo Navis (plate 32).

In astrology, Aries, as the first sign of the twelve, is seen as the great initiator, overthrowing the old order and establishing a new one in its place, just as Jason had to overthrow his wicked uncle and win the Golden Fleece. It is the sign of the original, creative, independent spirit, and the Ram was indeed worshipped as such in Egypt, where it was sacred to the king of the gods, Ammon, and in Greece, where it belonged to Zeus. In Israel it was sacrificed to Jehovah. Not only is it the first, and so the pioneer and leader of the zodiac, but it is also a fire sign, ruled by Mars, the god of war. On the plus side, Arians are considered to be brave, romantic, spontaneous and original, forever on a quest to give life new meaning, but they can be headstrong, prone to accidents and their tempers run on a short fuse.

The Stars

As the constellation of spring and the beginning of the year, Aries led the flocks of stars across the skies, and its most important star, Hamal, was known in Babylon as the Proclaimer of the Dawn and the Star of the Flocks.

To Locate

Aries, which is best seen in autumn and winter in the northern hemisphere, is a springtime constellation south of the equator. It lies between Pisces and Taurus on the zodiac band, and below Andromeda, with Cetus to the south.

MUSCA BOREALIS · THE FLY OF THE NORTH

The great Fly which has now, sadly, vanished from the modern star charts, was thought by some to represent Beelzebub who was the Syrian god Baal. To the Hebrews, however, he was a foreign god and so became for them a devil, second in command to Satan. Beelzebub has commonly been translated as the 'Lord of Flies'.

PLATE 17

TAURUS

the BULL

Between Aries and Gemini on the zodiac band lies Taurus, the great Babylonian 'Bull of Heaven', one of the most ancient symbols of fertility and power. On either side of him are the heroes, Perseus and Orion and, at his feet, the mighty river Eridanus, which flows down towards the southern pole.

Taurus, the white celestial bull, was placed in the heavens at the request of Ishtar, the barbaric Babylonian Venus. Gilgamesh, the world's first recorded hero, spurned her favours, accusing her of destroying all her lovers, which included lions and horses. In her rage, she flew up to heaven and forced her father Anu to create the 'Bull of Heaven' to destroy him. The sign of Taurus is ruled by Venus to this day.

Other Taurean myths include the story of Europa, who was seduced by Zeus in the form of a white bull. He swam out to sea with her, garlanded with flowers, and landed on the shores of Crete, where she gave birth to Minos, father of the monstrous Minotaur. Half bull, half man, he was conceived when Minos' wife was struck by the gods with a blind passion for a bull. Locked in the Labyrinth, he lived on human flesh until the Athenian hero Theseus, with the help of Ariadne's ball of thread, found him in the centre, killed him, and managed to retrace his steps to freedom. The myths of the minotaur in fact date from far earlier times in Crete, when the bull was sacred to the Great Goddess.

In astrology, Taurus is the first of the three earth signs, ruled, as we have seen, by the voluptuous planet Venus. After the zodiac's fiery, pioneering start in Aries, Taurus, the sign of the earth when it turns green in spring, concentrates on giving form and substance to what Aries has begun, and on enjoying the pleasures of this world. Taurus is a fixed sign, and its natives are seen as steady, reliable, loyal and warm-hearted, with all the strength and endurance of their symbol, but they can be stubborn and passionately possessive too.

The Stars

The great 'red giant', war-like Aldebaran, is the star of the Archangel Michael, one of the ancient 'key stars of the heavens', the 'Watcher in the East'. The oldest known zodiac was measured from it, and its rising in April marked the beginning of the Babylonian year. Because of this, it was known as the 'Forecaster' and the 'Star of the Tablet', and was sacred to the god Nabu, who inscribed on a tablet the decisions taken at the spring congress of the gods. The most important Druid festival also began when the sun entered the sign.

The Age of Taurus, which started around 4139 BC and ended in 1963 BC, saw the beginnings of a less nomadic life style in the Middle East. The Hyades, which herald rain, and the Pleiades, or the Seven Sisters, which promise fair weather, were the daughters of the giant Atlas, who supported the world on his shoulders, and which the mountains of Morocco may be named after. In the festival of Hallowe'en can be seen traces of the early worship of the dead, which was connected with the first rising of the Pleiades in November.

To Locate

To locate Taurus, which is an easy constellation to see clearly, follow the line of Orion's belt upwards during winter and early spring until you reach Aldebaran, the Eye of Taurus, surrounded by the V-shaped cluster of the Hyades, which makes up the Bull's face. The Pleiades are on its back. It can be seen between November and February south of the equator.

> ### PLATE 18
> # GEMINI
> *the* HEAVENLY TWINS

Castor and Pollux, the Heavenly Twins, lying between Cancer and Taurus on the zodiac band, were immortalised for brotherly love.

Zeus, in the shape of a dazzling white swan, seduced Leda, the wife of Tyndareus. The result of their union was two great eggs, one of which contained Helen of Troy and the immortal Pollux, who were the children of Zeus. In the other were the offspring of Tyndareus, the mortal Castor, and his sister Clytemnestra, who murdered her husband in the bath.

Castor, who was a famous horseman, and Pollux, who was a boxer, were inseparable. They accompanied the Argonauts on their famous journey and calmed the rough seas which threatened to capsize the boat. They have been an omen of good luck to sailors ever since and the appearance of twin balls of lightning in the rigging, which we now call St Elmo's Fire, after the fourth-century Syrian bishop Erasmus, who became the patron saint of sailors, was a guarantee of safety from the storm. A single light, however, presaged disaster, as this was Helen, the fateful sister of the twins, who had caused the fall of Troy.

The help of the Heavenly Twins was invoked in war as well as storm. In 496 BC, during the Roman war with Latium, the authorities decided to erect a temple to them, although up until then they had not been Roman gods. Within moments, the Twins appeared, leading the Roman cavalry to victory. That evening, two youths, both dressed in purple, were seen watering their white horses at a fountain in the Forum, and a huge temple in their honour was built without delay.

A symbol of duality, and of the coexistence of the mortal

and immortal sides of man, they spent alternate nights in Hades and Olympus, and they stood for Life and Death in Rome. Their origins, in fact, go back to the Euphrates.

In astrology, Gemini is an intellectual air sign, ruled by the quick-witted trickster, Mercury, the messenger of the gods, whom it was impossible to capture or pin down, and mercurial is the word which best describes the sign. Like the Heavenly Twins who divide their time between the gloomy underworld and the dizzy heights of Mount Olympus, Geminis are seen as volatile and moody. Endlessly curious, talkative and witty, they can get bored and restless when forced to face the duller, more mundane aspects of life. The goals of Gemini are to unite the opposites within them, and to come to terms with the human condition and its limitations. Like Mercury, the messenger, their domain is communication.

The Stars

Both Castor and Pollux are extremely bright stars, which have been recognised as twins not only in Europe and Asia, but by the Australian Aborigines and the Polynesians. Castor is an enormous 'multiple' star, which portended mischief and violence in astrology, while Pollux, the orange star of the immortal boxer, brought fame and glory.

To Locate

Take a line straight along the handle of the Plough and out through Merak, or from the bottom star of Orion through Betelgeux (or Betelgeuse) on his left shoulder to find Castor and Pollux. Gemini can be seen from November to April in the northern hemisphere, and from December to March south of the equator.

PLATE 19

CANCER

the CRAB

Cancer, the Crab, which lives on the shore of the ocean, is ruled by the waxing and waning moon, which was thought to be in Cancer at the time of the Creation.

The second labour of Hercules was to kill the many-headed Hydra, a monstrous water-snake which lived in the marshes of Lerna in Greece. Whenever he cut off one head, two grew in its place. In the battle in which he finally overcame it, all the animals were on his side except the crab, which snapped at his ankles, and which had been sent by his enemy, the queen of the gods. Both the moon and the sea, the source of all life, are symbols of the Great Mother, to whom the Crab belongs, and who resents the hero's bid for freedom from her thrall.

Although the stars of Cancer make up one of the most inconspicuous of the constellations, described as 'black and without eyes', it was of prime importance in the ancient world. Known as the Gate of Man, it was the doorway through which souls came down from heaven to be born into this world of flux and change ruled by the moon.

Cancer has always been seen as a hard-shelled animal. It was a tortoise in Babylon and the sacred scarab beetle of the sun god in ancient Egypt.

This is the first water sign and the fourth sign of the zodiac in astrology, and as creatures of the seashore, Cancerians are thought to be more in touch than almost any other sign with the wellsprings of life and the collective memories of mankind. Their ability to tap into that hidden wisdom and to pass it on is witnessed by the countless artists and writers born under Cancer. They are good parents and, ruled by the moon and the sea, which are both symbols of the mother, they have the gift for 'giving birth', both literally and to ideas, which makes the Gate of Man a very fitting symbol for the sign. Imagination, intuition, sensitivity and feeling are the hallmarks of the Cancerian personality, and their moods are said to change just like the tides. Because they are so sensitive and open, they tend to use their hard shells for protection, scuttling sideways out of danger and, like the crab sent to bite Hercules, they resent change and are nostalgic for the past.

The Stars

Although its stars are dim, Cancer boasts the famous Beehive Cluster in its centre. Also known as Praesepe, or the Manger, in which Christ, perhaps, was born – possibly because that was the Gate of Man – it is only visible to the naked eye as a fuzzy spot, but it is one of the closest star clusters in the sky. Like many clusters in astrology, it brought mischief and blindness in its train.

To Locate

Cancer is best seen in spring in the northern hemisphere, and in autumn in the south. It lies between Regulus in Leo to the east, Pollux in Gemini to the west and north of Procyon in Canis Minor.

PLATE 20

LEO MAJOR
the GREAT LION *and*
LEO MINOR
the LITTLE LION

The King of Beasts, now accompanied by the Little Lion, was one of the Four Guardians of the Heavens. Lying between Cancer and Virgo, it has always been associated with the sun and with the heat of summer.

LEO MAJOR · THE GREAT LION

The first labour of the great solar hero, Hercules, was to kill the Nemean Lion. It was sent from the moon by his enemy, Hera, the queen of heaven, and he strangled it with his bare hands. Its skin, which made him invincible, he wore from that day on.

The proud and passionate lion, a symbol of kingship and masculine power, was worshipped in ancient Egypt as the sun entered Leo at the time of the annual flooding of the Nile. Their reverence for its sacred, fertilising waters, and for the Lion which caused them, is the origin of the many lion-headed fountains, where the water flows from the lion's mouth.

The sphinx is thought by some to be made up of the body of Leo and the head of the neighbouring constellation, Virgo, who, in Egypt, was seen as the goddess Isis.

In astrology, Leo, a fire sign and ruled by the sun, is the proudest and most regal of the zodiac signs. On the positive side, its natives are said to be magnanimous, creative, enthusiastic and warm-hearted, but they can be pompous, bossy and dogmatic. Their sense of drama and their extrovert ways can be misleading, however, for there is a great deal more to Leo than the desire to hold the centre of the stage. Ruled by the Sun, which symbolises the true self, the real goal of Leo is the attainment of unique individuality. Hercules' battle with the Nemean Lion depicts the struggle to achieve it by overcoming the fiery passions of the heart. Having killed the lion, and triumphed over uncontrolled emotion, he can then wear the lion's skin which makes him king.

LEO MINOR · THE LITTLE LION

The Little Lion is a new invention, created in the seventeenth century. It has no real myths attached to it, although this part of the sky was thought, in ancient Egypt, to be sacred to the great god Ptah.

The Stars

Regulus, the Lion's Heart, described as 'white flushed ultramarine' in colour, has been the ruler of the heavens in many parts of Europe and Asia since around 4000 BC. One of the ancient Persians' Four Guardians of the Heavens, it was the star of riches, glory and power.

Denebola, the Lion's Tail, was as unlucky as Regulus was lucky, bringing disgrace and misfortune. The shower of shooting stars known as the Leonids, reach their peak around 17 November. These can, occasionally, turn into a meteor storm, falling at the rate of 100,000 every hour.

To Locate

The famous reverse question mark of Leo dominates the southern sky in spring in the northern hemisphere, and the northern sky in autumn south of the equator.

The winged Virgin, holding the palm branch and the Ear of Wheat which marks her brightest star, was worshipped as the great goddess of the harvest throughout the ancient world.

The origins of the cult of the Great Goddess, who was both virgin and mother, are prehistoric, but since the dawn of recorded history she has been associated with the constellation Virgo, through which the sun passes around harvest-time.

She is the ancient Iraqi goddess Ishtar, Queen of the Stars, the lover of the corn god Tammuz, whose death she mourns every autumn, when he is cut down in his prime. Winter reigns during her journey to the underworld to bring him back, after which he reappears as the new, green corn each spring.

The stories of Venus and Adonis, of Isis and Osiris, and of Cybele, the early Asiatic goddess in her turreted crown who loved Attis, are all variations on the theme. As Virgo follows Leo on the zodiac band, the chariot of Cybele is drawn by lions.

In Greece, Virgo is Demeter, the goddess of the corn, as well as her daughter Persephone, who spends the winter in the underworld and returns to earth each spring. Virgo is also the muse of astronomy, Urania, who was believed to have been placed in the skies by Apollo, the god of music and prophecy.

To the Romans she was Astraea, the goddess of justice and of the laws of nature, who was the last of the immortals to leave 'the blood-soaked earth' after the Gold, Silver and Bronze Ages gave way to the wickedness of modern times and the Age of Iron. Her promised return, and the imminent birth of a child who would restore the Golden Age, made it easy for the Christians to see Virgo as the Virgin Mary.

In astrology, Virgo belongs to the element of earth and is ruled by the intellectual planet Mercury, which were both allotted to it in the second century AD. This combination fostered the idea of 'practical mind' and so the ancient goddess of fertility and the harvest slowly changed into the Ideal Secretary, the tidy analytical perfectionist, which is the classic but misleading image of the sign today. The real nature and meaning of Virgo lies in the matriarchal virgin goddess of the distant past, who was later turned into the Virgin Mary. A symbol not of chastity, but of synthesis and wholeness, she was a virgin because she was independent, free and self-contained.

The Stars

Spica, the Ear of Wheat, is Virgo's most important star, and the famous temple to the many-breasted Diana of Ephesus, in Turkey, was built in alignment with it. Virgo, seen lying on her back with her feet towards the east, is now known as the 'realm of the galaxies', as around 3000 of them, about sixty-five light years distant, are scattered over the head and shoulders and the left wing of the goddess like dim jewels. Her Gamma star, between her left upper arm and her waist on the card, Porrima, was a Roman goddess of prophecy. Vindemiatrix, the Grape Gatherer, which marks her right arm, is so called because its morning rising occurs just before the vintage.

To Locate

Virgo lies between Leo and Libra, with Boötes to the north and Hydra to the south. It is best seen in spring and summer in the northern hemisphere, and in autumn and winter south of the equator. Draw an imaginary arc on down from the curved handle of the Plough, Ursa Major, to find Arcturus in Boötes and then Spica in Virgo.

PLATE 22

LIBRA

the SCALES

Libra, the Golden Scales which lie halfway round the zodiac band between the Virgin Goddess and the Scorpion, is an age-old symbol of justice, harmony and balance.

The Romans claimed to have created Libra from the ancient Scorpion's claws. They gave the scales to Astraea, the goddess of justice, who left the earth in disgust and now shines in the sky as Virgo, but their true origin dates back to around 2000 BC. For this was the season of the year in Babylon which was connected with the weighing of souls and with the judgement of the living and the dead. Day and night are equal at the autumn equinox, when the sun passes through Libra, and the zodiac, and the year, and so men's souls are in the balance. Although they glittered in the skies of ancient Egypt, their presence was not again recorded until they were mysteriously reinvented by the star-gazers of Rome. In between, these stars were seen as the Scorpion's claws.

The stars of Libra were also seen as an altar on a mound, connected with the Tower of Babel, in the distant past, and as the lighthouse of Alexandria, one of the Seven Wonders of the World, which appeared as a great lamp clasped between the Scorpion's claws.

In astrology, Libra is the second of the intellectual air signs, but unlike Gemini, which is ruled by quick-witted Mercury, it is governed by Venus, the goddess of love. The main concerns of those born under Libra, which is the only abstract symbol amongst the zodiac of living beings, are believed to be inner balance and harmonious relationships with others, which their Venusian love of beauty and romance, and their charm and sense of justice help them to achieve. Falling in love with love can be a problem, though, as like one half of a pair of scales, they need other people to feel balanced, and they will do almost anything not to live alone. They are seen as the diplomats of the zodiac, but their ability to understand both sides of a situation can lead to endless indecision.

The Stars

Libra's second star, Zubeneschimali, is one of the only green stars in the sky which can be seen clearly without a telescope. The round pattern of the constellation was thought to represent the circular altar of early times.

To Locate

Libra, which lies between Virgo and Scorpio on the celestial zodiac, is north of Centaurus and south of the head of Serpens. It is best seen in summer in the northern hemisphere and in autumn and winter in the South.

The great Scorpion of the zodiac lies between Libra, which once made up its claws, and the wild centaur, Sagittarius, who aims his arrow at its heart.

As the hunter, Orion, sets each spring in the west his enemy, the Scorpion, rises in the eastern sky. For this is the Scorpion who, at the command of Artemis, the chaste goddess of hunting and the moon, stung the handsome Orion and caused his death, from which even Asclepius, the god of healing, could not save him. The Scorpion was also thought to have stung the horses of the sun god's chariot when Phaeton drove them, causing them to bolt and career through the heavens, drying up rivers and scorching the earth below.

But the Scorpion was really formed in about 5000 BC in the Euphrates valley, where it was sacred to the god of war and was a symbol of the darkness and decay of the waning year. Gilgamesh, the prototype of all our heroes, was challenged by a scorpion-man who guarded the gates of the sunrise, which were great folding doors in the steep side of the mountains of the East.

It has always been greatly feared by sailors, as its autumn setting promised storms. For the alchemists, however, who believed that they could produce gold by releasing the spirit from its bondage in matter, November, Scorpio's season, when the earth decays, was their busiest time of year. Only then could the spirit be released, and base metal be transmuted into gold.

In astrology, it was the 'baleful source of war and discord' in medieval times, when the birthplace of its ruler, the war-like planet Mars, was located in its sting. Today it gets a slightly better press as the sign of sex, death, transformation and rebirth, ruled over by the powerful planet Pluto. Scorpios are considered passionate, intense, determined and loyal, but on their dark side, with which they have to battle, they can be self-destructive as the scorpion shows, jealous, cynical and vindictive. The story of the scorpionic Faust and the mocking Mephistopheles, to whom he sold his soul, show bitterness and cynicism as the root of Scorpio's troubles, but the soaring eagle, which is the other symbol of the sign, shows the heights to which it can attain once it has won the fight. It is a fixed water sign.

The Stars

The great, red heart of Scorpio, Antares, 'the rival of Mars', was one of the Persian Royal Stars in 3000 BC, and is the Chinese 'Heart of the Green Dragon'. Antares, like the other red 'supergiant', Betelgeux (or Betelgeuse) in Orion, which rises as it sets, portends war and martial honours. It is surrounded by a huge red nebula, invisible to the naked eye, and is 700 times larger, and 9000 times brighter than our sun. North of the Scorpion's tail lies the famous Butterfly star cluster, appearing to the naked eye as a fuzzy patch half the diameter of the full moon.

To Locate

Scorpio lies between Hydra and Serpentarius (now Ophiuchus), but most of its stars are invisible from the northern hemisphere. Antares can be seen on summer evenings, a great, red star low on the horizon to the south. It is high in the northern sky during the winter in the southern hemisphere.

PLATE 24

SAGITTARIUS
the ARCHER *and*

CORONA AUSTRALIS
the SOUTHERN CROWN *with*

MICROSCOPIUM
and TELESCOPIUM

SAGITTARIUS *and* CORONA AUSTRALIS

The heavenly Archer, Sagittarius, stands with his bow drawn back, his arrow pointing at Antares, the star which marks the Scorpion's heart.

The famous horsemen of Thessaly in Greece, who were the first cowboys, rounding up their cattle on the plains, are thought perhaps to be the origin of the centaurs. Greek mythology, however, gives them a different start. There, they are the offspring of a cloud which took the form of Hera, the queen of heaven, and of Ixion, who was banished to the underworld by Zeus to spin for ever on a burning wheel for boasting that he could win Hera's love.

With the exception of Chiron, who was wise and good and taught several of the Greek heroes the mysteries of life, they were a savage, cruel and drunken lot, who drew the chariot of Bacchus, the orgiastic god of wine, and were bent on rape and pillage. Their real origin, however, is thought by some to lie much further back in the Gandharvas, the celestial horsemen of ancient India. Corona Australis, the centaur's wreath at Sagittarius' feet, which was often portrayed as a crown, is a memory of the golden sun rays which emanated from the horses' heads.

Sagittarius also formed part of the original Babylonian zodiac, where he was their archer god of war.

In astrology, Sagittarius is the last of the fire signs and is ruled by Jupiter, the luckiest planet in the sky. Coming after Scorpio, the sign of death and regeneration, Sagittarius is thought to be an optimistic, forward-looking sign. Jupiter, as king of the gods, represents the eternal spirit, and the goal of Sagittarius is therefore nothing less than discovering the meaning of existence, so religion and philosophy play a large part in their lives. New horizons beckon and life is an adventure in which the journey is almost more important than the goal. Cheerful, freedom-loving, direct and open-minded, the Sagittarian character can also be restless and refuse to face responsibility. They may have no time for petty detail, but they can draw on the energy and wisdom of nature and the instincts embodied in their centaur side to aim their arrow at the stars.

The Stars

The centre of our galaxy is in Sagittarius on the shoulder of the Large Sagittarius Star Cloud near the border of Scorpio. This is one of the areas of the heavens most densely populated with nebulae and stars, which can be seen with the naked eye. It is now thought that at the heart of the galaxy there may be an enormous black hole, probably as heavy as a thousand suns.

MICROSCOPIUM AND TELESCOPIUM

Microscopium and Telescopium were both invented in 1752 by Nicolas La Caille.

To Locate

To find Sagittarius, locate Antares on the horizon during the northern summer, and then look to the east, at the same height above the horizon. In the southern hemisphere it is on view during the winter in the northern sky.

PLATE 25

CAPRICORNUS
the GOAT-FISH

2500 years ago the sun reached its nadir at the winter solstice and then began its slow climb towards midsummer, in the sign of Capricorn, the Goat-Fish, one of the most mysterious and ancient symbols in the skies. For the Goat-Fish, known in pre-Babylonian times as 'The Antelope of the Subterranean Ocean', is the god Ea, 'He of the vast intellect', 'Lord of the Sacred Eye'.

Records from the library of Ashurbanipal in Nineveh, around 600 BC, describe the ancient Sumerian vision of the world. The earth, a round plateau ringed with mountains, which supported the domed sky, floated on the sweet, primordial waters, which broke through the earth's surface as fresh water springs. The Tigris and Euphrates, the great rivers which watered the 'cradle of civilisation', the Chaldean plain, gushed up from the domain of the Goat-Fish, which was the source of all knowledge and wisdom. Near his earthly palace by the Persian gulf grew a mighty tree, whose leaves and branches shone like lapis lazuli, and which cast as much shade as a whole forest.

Ea was the only one amongst the ancient gods who was always kind and never angry, and he is responsible for saving mankind from the Flood. The story in which he tells the Sumerian Noah, Uta-Napishtim, to build an ark, is much the same as the Bible's version of the great disaster. He is also said to have emerged four times, at long intervals, from the subterranean ocean to teach men the arts of civilisation. When he appears, it is in human form, wearing a fish-tailed cloak. After educating mankind, he returns to the waters as darkness falls.

It was only in later times that Capricorn became an earth sign and was associated with the Greek goat god, Pan. In astrology, Capricorn is ruled by Saturn. Its symbol, the mysterious creature which is half-goat, half-fish, reveals a lot about the dual Capricornian nature. On the one hand, it is the goat which climbs the steep mountain of success; ambitious, cautious, sure-footed and hard-working. On the other, and this side tends to get forgotten, it is the fish which swims in the deep waters, in touch with the great ocean of the psyche, and a lot deeper, more sensitive and introverted than it seems.

On the dark side, as it is ruled by Saturn, the old and rigid king, it can be stern and moralistic. As the sign which dominates the cold and barren winter solstice, when the days start to get longer, Capricorn was the traditional sign in which the sun gods and redeemers were reborn to suffer the human lot and lead man to the light. Capricornians are said to often choose what may appear to be a harsh fate, nailed, as it were, to the cross of matter, but their real motives are responsibility to others and a deep compassion.

To Locate

Capricorn is in the ocean-oriented part of the northern autumnal sky, along with Aquarius, the water bearer, the Whale, the Dolphin, the Southern Fish, and the two fish of the zodiac sign of Pisces. It can be seen in early autumn, reaching its highest point at 10 p.m. on 1 September. In the northern hemisphere, it is low above the southern horizon. From the southern hemisphere, it is high in the northern sky in spring.

PLATE 26

AQUARIUS
the WATER BEARER
PISCIS AUSTRALIS
the SOUTHERN FISH *and*
BALLON
AEROSTATIQUE
the HOT AIR BALLOON

AQUARIUS · THE WATER BEARER

Aquarius, the Water Bearer, is one of the oldest constellations, standing with his foot on the head of the great Southern Fish, into whose mouth his waters pour.

Not much is known about Aquarius, except that he ruled over a huge area of the sky known as the Sea in ancient Babylon. Here are gathered: the Southern Fish; the Dolphin; the zodiac Fishes; Hydra, the Water Serpent; Capricorn, the Goat-Fish; the mighty river Eridanus, and Cetus, the sea monster. Together these make up the constellations of the fertilising 'Upper Waters' of the sky, which were seen as the source of life, through which the sun passed during the rainy season.

Aquarius' appearance has remained unchanged since the earliest times, although sometimes the water flowed directly from his hands and arms. In his hand he holds 'Norma Nilotica', a rod for measuring the rising waters of the Nile.

In astrology, Aquarius is the last of the three intellectual air signs, and is ruled by Uranus, which will be the planet of the new Aquarian Age. Uranus, which is named after the ancient Greek sky god, is the awakener, the planet which symbolises sudden change, flashes of insight and freedom, breaking down old structures to make way for the new. Those born under its influence are seen as original, inventive, idealistic and have a progressive, humanitarian outlook on life. They love freedom and hate to be tied down, but they can be stubborn when it comes to changing their own opinions. Unconventional, they can become eccentric and rebellious, living life on a high wire, but their gentler and more generous side has more in common with the god who pours out the heavenly waters for mankind.

The Stars

Aquarius' most important star, Sad el Melik, 'the lucky one of the king', marks his right shoulder just above the Urn and Sadalsuud, 'the luckiest of the lucky', lies on his upper left arm. Astrologers and astronomers disagree about when the 'New Age' of Aquarius, when the spring equinox moves out of Pisces, will begin. Astrologers divide the zodiac band into twelve equal portions, and by their reckoning, depending on which star is chosen as a marker, it could be any time between 1997 and 2200. Astronomers, however, claim that this will not happen for 600 years.

PISCIS AUSTRALIS · THE SOUTHERN FISH

The Southern Fish is sometimes thought to be the parent of the two well-known fishes which make up Pisces in the zodiac. It is connected with the early god, Oannes, who had a fish's body and human hands and feet. He is another version of the Capricornian Goat-Fish who was responsible for teaching man the arts and sciences, which he did by day, but his nights were spent in the depths of the Persian Gulf.

The Stars

4000 years ago in Persia, Fomalhaut, which marks the Fish's Mouth, was a Royal Star and one of the Four Guardians of the Heavens. The most southerly star on view from Britain, it is thought to have been worshipped at dawn at the Greek temple at Eleusis, and portended good fortune and power.

To Locate

Aquarius lies between Pisces and Capricorn, with the Southern Fish below it, and Pegasus to the north. The easiest stars to recognise are the ones which make up the Urn, which were immortalised by Van Gogh. It can be seen in autumn in the northern hemisphere and in spring in the south.

BALLON AEROSTATIQUE

Ballon Aerostatique is no longer included in the star charts of today. It was invented by the astronomer Lalande in 1798.

The two fishes of Pisces, the last sign of the zodiac, swim in different directions, but bound by a cord, between Aries, the Ram, and Aquarius, the Water Carrier.

The fishes are both a Christian and a pagan symbol. They first appear in an early myth, pushing a giant egg out of the waters of the river Euphrates. From the egg emerged the love-goddess Atagartis. Both she and her son-lover, Ichthys, took the form of fishes and in all her temples there were sacred fish ponds. This early fish cult, which centres around the mother goddess and her son, who dies annually and is reborn, has many things in common with the Christian story, and Christ, the Fisher of Men who divided the loaves and the fishes, was known as Ichthys, which means Fish, in early Christian times.

The beginning of the Age of the Fishes, when the spring equinox moved on after its 2000-year stay in Aries into Pisces, roughly coincided with Christ's birth, now dated by most people at around 7 BC. In that year, Jupiter and Saturn met, at the point marking the new Piscean equinox in the skies, making one exceptionally bright star which, in the winter months, could have guided the three Wise Men due south from Jerusalem to Bethlehem.

In astrology, Pisces is a water sign and ruled by Neptune. Pisces is considered to be the most mystically inclined of all the signs and, as the last of the twelve, it represents the return to the great ocean from which life first evolved, and where all boundaries are dissolved. Often dreamy and diffuse, they are seen as also being gentle, creative, intuitive and sensitive. So much so, in fact, that they can see themselves as victims, but their ability to sympathise and empathise with others makes them equally capable of living out the saviour side of the Pisces myth.

The Stars

El Rischa, the cord, which is Pisces' leading star, marks the knot which ties the Fish together. The nearest star to Aries, it was here that the planetary meeting happened in 7 BC, which could have marked the birth of Christ.

To Locate

Best seen between October and December in the northern hemisphere, the 'circlet' of Pisces, which is the head of the Western Fish, lies just to the south of the 'Great Square of Pegasus'. South of the equator, they are on view in spring.

<table>
<tr><td colspan="2" align="center">PLATE 28</td></tr>
</table>

PSALTERIUM GEORGII	OFFICINA SCULPTORIS
FLUVIUS ERIDANUS *the* RIVER ERIDANUS	FORNAX CHEMICA *and*
CETUS *the* WHALE *or* SEA MONSTER	MACHINA ELECTRICA

FLUVIUS ERIDANUS

The river Eridanus is named after the river god who was the son of Oceanus, the great River of Time which encircled the earth. It was into the Eridanus, which welled up from the timeless Islands of the Blessed, that Phaeton plunged to his death when he fell from the Sun's chariot. His sisters, the Heliades, who buried him, were transformed into poplar trees and their tears turned into amber, which lay everywhere along its banks. The longest constellation in the sky, Eridanus, the River of Night, was also the sky image of the Nile and the Euphrates, once thought to be two parts of one great river which was associated with Paradise and Eden.

The Stars

Eridanus' brightest star Achernar, the End of the River, is a blue giant. It is the ninth brightest in the sky, and is about 120 light-years distant. (See map.)

To Locate

The Northern Stream of Eridanus flows from Rigel in Orion

down to Cetus. The Southern Stream runs from Cetus down to Achernar, which lies near the southern Phoenix, and which can only be seen from south of 30° north. It is a late autumn constellation in the northern hemisphere, and can best be seen from the southern hemisphere in spring.

CETUS · THE WHALE OR SEA MONSTER

In Cetus the Greeks saw the great sea monster sent to devour Andromeda, but which Perseus turned to stone. (See Perseus, Plate 6.) What was thought to be its forty foot long skeleton, with vertebrae six foot in circumference, was brought to ancient Rome, where it was much marvelled at. Cetus lies in the area of the skies known as the Sea in ancient Babylon, where it is thought to have represented Tiamat, the she-dragon of chaos, who personified the ocean and the source of life. Overcome by Marduk, who stood for cosmic order, Tiamat has now been 'reinstated on her throne' after 4000 years by the new school of 'Chaos' mathematicians who, since the 1970s, have found creative pattern in apparent chaos and who no longer see it as the 'enemy' of order.

The Stars

On the neck of the sea-beast is Mira, 'the Wonderful', the most famous of the variable stars which fluctuate in size, near a group of stars known by the Chinese as Heaven's Sewer.

To Locate

The fourth largest constellation in the sky, Cetus lies south of Pisces and east of Aquarius. (See Eridanus.)

THE OTHER CONSTELLATIONS ON THIS CARD

PSALTERIUM GEORGII was created by Maximillian Hell to glorify George II of England and has been removed from modern sky charts. FORNAX CHEMICA was invented in the mid-eighteenth century and is called 'Heaven's Temporary Granary' by the Chinese; and OFFICINA SCULPTORIS and MACHINA ELECTRICA, both quite recent creations, have now also been discarded.

PLATE 29

O R I O N

the HUNTER

Orion, the heavenly Hunter in his golden armour, club in hand and holding a trophy from the chase, shines on the celestial equator, through which runs his belt, the String of Pearls. At his feet, although they are not shown on the same card, are Lepus, the Hare and the Dog Star, Sirius, in Canis Major.

The legendary Orion was not only the most beautiful man the world has ever known, but a giant so tall that he could wade through any sea with his head above the waters – when he was not hunting with his dogs in the wooded hills of Greece. He has a stormy reputation, and has long been a star of ill-omen among sailors, as the evening rising of his handsome head above the eastern ocean coincides, in the northern hemisphere, with the start of winter and bad weather.

The stories which describe the great Hunter's exploits echo the annual rising and setting of his stars. His first marriage ended when his boastful wife was banished to the underworld, but his chequered career, which ended in the stars, had only just begun. His blinding by the jealous father of his next love, who was a Greek princess, reflects, perhaps, his springtime setting in the west. His annual reappearance in the eastern sky in autumn, is also echoed by the story of the oracle which told him to travel east and gaze into the sunrise to regain his sight. As he looked at Aurora, the goddess of the dawn and the mother of the winds and of the Morning Star, she fell in love with him, and Orion, who had been blind all summer, could see the world once more.

As the Scorpion rises in the summer sky each spring, Orion fades, and it is from a scorpion's sting, inflicted by Artemis, the angry virgin goddess of hunting and the moon, who also loved him, that the beautiful Orion meets his end. After his 'death', he hunts on in the underworld and is then placed in the heavens with the Dog Star, Sirius, beside him. There, with his sight and life restored, he glitters in the evening sky throughout the winter.

In Babylon, the brilliant constellation of Orion was worshipped as the god who created precious stones.

The Stars

The rich topaz-coloured Betelgeux (or Betelgeuse), known to Arab astronomers as the Armpit of the Central One, marks the right shoulder of the Hunter. It rises in the autumn skies as Antares, the red heart of the Scorpion which killed Orion, sets. Portending fortune, wealth and martial honours, this red supergiant, which fluctuates in size, could contain the entire orbit of the earth around the sun.

Rigel, the Mariner's Star, is the Giant's Leg, the brightest in Orion and the seventh brightest in the sky. It is a blue-white supergiant, 57,000 times more luminous than our sun. Bellatrix, the Conqueror, or the Amazon Star, marks his left shoulder.

The three bright stars which make up his belt are Anilam, Alnitak and Mintaka. They are also known as the Magi, the Three Wise Men from the East, who travelled west to the Holy Land, following the star which marked the birth of Christ and, like the Magi, they travel westwards through the autumn skies towards Pisces, where the star appeared.

To Locate

Turn towards the south in winter in the northern hemisphere to find Orion, which is the brightest constellation in the sky. His belt is a well-known 'pointer' to many other constellations. Study the description of the winter sky, pp. 9-15. From the southern hemisphere, it is visible from October to March, but upside- down.

PLATE 30

CANIS MAJOR
the GREAT DOG

LEPUS
the HARE

COLUMBA NOACHI
NOAH'S DOVE *and*

CELA SCULPTORIS
the SCULPTOR'S TOOL

CANIS MAJOR · THE GREAT DOG

The Great Dog follows his master, Orion, as he makes his annual journey through the sky, forever pursuing the Hare at his feet. In olden times, the Dog Star, Sirius, was more important than the Dog himself, who is sometimes called the Keeper of Hell, 'the watch dog of the lower heavens'. It is also linked with Anubis, the dog-headed god of ancient Egypt, who accompanies the soul on its 'night sea-crossing' after death.

The Stars

The Dog Star, Sirius, is the brightest in the heavens, and its name means 'sparkling' and 'scorching' as it is nearest to the sun during the height of summer. The hot, enervating Dog Days, which Sirius was thought to cause, run from 3 July to 11 August.

The Dog appears on Mesopotamian temples and mounds, and was worshipped in Egypt as long ago as 3285 BC, as Sirius rose when the Nile flooded. In Greece, the Eleusinian mysteries are thought to have celebrated its culmination at midnight, and Roman farmers sacrificed a fawn-coloured dog to it each year to ensure a good harvest. A Finnish myth describes how two star-lovers, Zulamith the Bold, and Salami the Fair, fell into each other's arms, thus explaining its enormous size.

Mirzam, the Announcer, which marks the Dog's Paw, is so called because it rises just before Sirius. Some say that it was also called Isis, after the great Egyptian goddess.

To Locate

The three stars of Orion's Belt point at the Dog Star, Sirius, in Canis Major at Orion's heels. It is so bright that it is hard to miss, and is best seen in winter, between December and March in the northern hemisphere (see pp. 9-10), and between November and April in the southern hemisphere (see pp. 15-16).

LEPUS · THE HARE

At the feet of Orion, the mighty Hunter, lies Lepus, the Hare, pursued by the Great Dog. It was first named by the Greeks of the island of Sicily, 'the country noted in early days for the great devastation by hares'. Orion is a solar hero, and the hare has long been associated with the moon. In Japan, the markings on the moon's face are known as the Jewelled Hare.

The Stars

The four brightest stars in Lepus were known to the Arab astronomers as the 'thirst-slaking Camels', as they are near the waters of the Milky Way. Hind's Crimson Star, described by its discoverer as 'a drop of blood on a black field', can only be seen with a telescope, but is one of the reddest in the sky.

COLUMBA NOACHI · NOAH'S DOVE

This is a modern constellation, placed in the skies in 1679, as is CELA SCULPTORIS, now known as CELA, which was created in 1750.

```
┌─────────────────────────────────────────┐
│              ▌PLATE 31▐                   │
│                                           │
│          CANIS  MINOR                     │
│          the LITTLE DOG and               │
│          MONOCEROS                        │
│          the UNICORN and                  │
│    ATELIER  TYPOGRAPHIQUE                  │
└─────────────────────────────────────────┘
```

CANIS MINOR · THE LITTLE DOG

The Little Dog, which now stands on the back of the Unicorn, is the second of Orion's hunting dogs. It has been associated with the dogs which tore the unsuspecting Actaeon to pieces when he came upon Artemis, the virgin goddess of the hunt, bathing in a woodland pool, and with the Egyptian dog-headed god, Anubis, the guide of souls. It was also the favourite dog of Helen of Troy, whose prayers for its immortality were answered when it was placed among the stars.

The Stars

Its main star, Procyon, which means 'Before the Dog', rises just before Sirius in Canis Major. It is a very fortunate star, known to the Mesopotamians as 'The Star of the Crossing of the Water - Dog', as it lies near their River of Heaven, the Milky Way.

MONOCEROS · THE UNICORN

Monoceros, the Unicorn, was not invented until 1690 and has no legends attached to it, but it does boast the two most massive stars yet discovered, each estimated to be fifty-five times the mass of our sun. Two great blue supergiants that revolve around each other, they are located on the head of the Unicorn, and known as Plaskett's Star.

To Locate

Take a line from Bellatrix, on Orion's left shoulder, through Betelgeux (or Betelgeuse) on his left, out to Procyon and Monoceros. From the northern hemisphere, Procyon can be seen between November and April in the southern sky. South of the equator, it is in the northern sky between December and April. Procyon, Sirius in Canis Major and Rigel, the star that marks Orion's foot, form a bright right angle in the sky.

ATELIER TYPOGRAPHIQUE

This was created by the astronomer Bode around 1800, but no longer features on star charts.

PLATE 32

N O C T U A	**L U P U S**
the OWL	*the* WOLF
C O R V U S	**C E N T A U R U S**
the CROW	*the* CENTAUR
C R A T E R	**A N T L I A**
the CUP	**P N E U M A T I C A**
S E X T A N S U R A N I A E	*the* AIR PUMP
the SEXTANT	**A R G O N A V I S**
H Y D R A	*the* SHIP OF THE
the WATER SERPENT	ARGONAUTS *and*
F E L I S	**P Y X I S N A U T I C A**
the CAT	*the* COMPASS

NOCTUA · THE OWL

The Owl is a relatively recent invention, which has now been removed from modern maps of the heavens.

CORVUS · THE CROW

Although it is now known as a crow this is, in fact, the prophetic raven of Apollo. The silver feathers of this all-seeing bird were turned forever black when it was cursed by the angry god for being the bearer of the bad news that his mistress, Coronis, was unfaithful. For the Celts, the raven was also the sacred bird of Bran, the god whose prophesying head is said to be buried beneath the Tower of London, which is still guarded by ravens, upon whom the safety of the city is supposed to depend. Two ravens called Hugin and Mugin, or Mind and Memory, also sit on the shoulders of the Norse god, Odin, and inform him of everything that happens in the world. Its earliest appearance in the skies, however, seems to date back to the Euphrates valley, where it was one of the giant ravens bred by the dragon of chaos, Tiamat, or the Hydra, upon whose back it stands.

The Stars

Just between Corvus and Virgo lies the Sombrero galaxy, which looks like a cross between a hat and a flying saucer.

CRATER · THE CUP

In ancient Greece, Crater, the golden goblet on the Hydra's back, belonged, like the raven Corvus, to the god of prophecy and poetic inspiration, Apollo, and to Dionysus, the ecstatic god of wine who, with his entourage of leopards, centaurs and satyrs, took Greece by storm from Asia Minor. It has also been connected with the 'Soma Cup' of ancient India and with the 'Cup of Christ', the Holy Grail.

SEXTANS URANIAE · THE SEXTANT

Sextans Uraniae is a seventeenth-century constellation named after the sextant with which the famous astronomer, Hevelius, made his calculations of the stars.

HYDRA · THE WATER SERPENT

The largest constellation in the sky, it represented the great dragon of chaos, Tiamat, in early Babylonian mythology, and was the 'Source of the Fountains of the Great Deep'. In China, it was the 'Red Bird' which governed the planets, and which was worshipped at the summer solstice as the symbol of immortality.

The Stars

Alphard, the Solitary One, marks the Hydra's heart.

FELIS · THE CAT

Felis is no longer included in modern star charts, but was created by the astronomer Lalande who, having been perplexed by the stars throughout his life, and being very fond of cats, announced that he would now have his joke and let the Cat scratch the 'starry chart'.

LUPUS · THE WOLF

The Wolf was known to the Greeks just as a wild animal, which the Centaur is carrying on his spear as a sacrifice to the gods. To the Arab astronomers of the Middle Ages it was Al Asadah, the Lioness, but to the ancient inhabitants of the Euphrates valley it was Zibu, the Beast, and Urbat, the Beast of Death, or the Star of the Dead Fathers.

CENTAURUS · THE CENTAUR

The story of the great centaur, Chiron, the legendary creator of the constellations, was thought, even by Sir Isaac Newton, to have at least some historic truth behind it.

Unlike most centaurs, including the war-like Sagittarius, Chiron, the 'founder of civilisation', was noble-looking, wise and kind-hearted. From Apollo and from Diana, he was the first to learn the arts of botany and medicine and of astronomy and music, and he could foretell the future from the stars. He was the teacher of several Greek heroes, including the young Achilles, to whom he passed on the secrets '...of the Gods, the stars/The tides' (Matthew Arnold, *Empedocles on Etna*), and of Hercules, one of whose poisoned arrows accidentally wounded him. Afraid that his wound would never heal, as he was immortal, he exchanged fates with Prometheus, who was chained to a rock for stealing fire from the gods and giving it to Man, and from there he was transferred to the stars.

It was Chiron who brought up Asclepius, the Greek god of healing, and taught him the mysteries of medicines and herbs (see Serpentarius, plate 12), and it was in his cave as children that Jason, Hercules, Hylas the Fair, the Heavenly Twins Castor and Pollux, and Orpheus the legendary musician, who later grew up into the Argonauts, first made friends and were taught by him to shoot, to sing and to tell the truth. (See Argo Navis for the story of the journey of the Argonauts.)

The Stars

Alpha Centauri, the Centaur's most important star, lies only 4.3 light years away from our solar system and is the closest star to our sun. It is, in fact, three stars, although to the naked eye it looks like one, and is the third brightest in the sky.

ANTLIA PNEUMATICA · THE AIR PUMP

The constellation of the Air Pump was invented in 1763 by the astronomer La Caille, who was the first person to map the southern skies, which he did from the Cape of Good Hope.

ARGO NAVIS · THE SHIP OF THE ARGONAUTS

The enormous constellation of Argo Navis has now been divided into Carina, the Keel; Puppis, the Stern; and Vela, the Sail, for the sake of convenience.

Although it was seen in ancient Egypt as the boat which carried Isis and Osiris over the deluge, it has been known since classical times as the great ship of the Argonauts, and the story of how Jason, with the help of the fifty Argonauts and the sorceress, Medea, whose chariot was drawn by dragons, sailed in it to win the Golden Fleece, is one of the most famous of the old Greek myths.

Sent by his wicked uncle, who had usurped his throne, to bring back the fleece, which hung in a sacred grove, guarded by a dragon in distant Colchis, Jason summoned all his childhood friends, who had now grown into heroes. The ship they built contained a branch from the prophetic 'speaking oak' of Dodona in its prow to guide them in their travels, which first took them past a land inhabited by six-handed giants, and then on to Asia Minor. Here, Hercules' friend, the beautiful youth, Hylas, was drawn to a watery death by the river nymphs who fell in love with him and, although Hercules searched the countryside and called for him, Hylas' answer from the depths of the stream was too faint for him to hear. Their journey took them next between clashing rocks which wandered in the sea 'like living things', and past the place where Prometheus was forever chained and tormented by an eagle for stealing the gods' fire, to Colchis, where they walked up to the city through a wood where dead men hung from all the trees. There Jason met Medea, the king's daughter, who fell in love with him, and helped him to win the fleece, and then fled back with the Argonauts to Greece.

Because they murdered Medea's brother to prevent him from raising the alarm, however, they were never destined to find peace and ten years later, when Jason fell in love with another woman, Medea killed the children she had borne him in a fit of jealousy and revenge.

The Stars

Canopus, Argo Navis' most important star, which is now in the new constellation of Carina, is a white supergiant used for spacecraft navigation and is the second brightest in the sky. It has always been associated with navigation and is named after Canopus, the pilot of the Greek fleet which sailed to Troy, who died near Alexandria on his way home. He gave his name both to the star and to the ancient city, now in ruins, where Nelson fought the Battle of the Nile and where the astronomer Ptolemy first recorded the outline of the ancient constellations from the terrace of the temple of Serapis in the second century AD.

To the Arabs, Canopus was the source of the colour in jewels. It was worshipped in the desert and was revered in Egypt, where it represented the god of the waters, and heralded the sunrise on the autumn equinox from a series of temples oriented towards it, which were built in 6400 BC. It is 200,000 times brighter than our sun.

Naos, in Puppis, is one of the hottest known stars, with a surface temperature of approximately 35,000°C.

PYXIS NAUTICA · THE COMPASS

Created by the astronomer La Caille in the 1750s, this little constellation's only claim to fame is that it contains the nova, or erupting star, which has flared more often than any other, and can be expected to do so again.

To Locate

This whole group of constellations is really best seen from the southern hemisphere, where it dominates the southern sky from January until May. From the northern hemisphere, it can be seen easily from the latitude of Egypt and the southern United States. Hydra, Crater and Corvus are more easily seen from northern latitudes than is Argo Navis, which is marked on modern star maps as the distinct constellations of CARINA, VELA and PUPPIS.